TRINA HAHNEMANN

The Scandinavian Cookbook

PHOTOGRAPHY BY LARS RANEK

Andrews McMeel
Publishing, LLC
Kansas City

First published in 2008 by Quadrille Publishing Limited, Alhambra
House, 27-31 Charing Cross Road, London WC2H 0LS

Text © 2008 by Trina Hahnemann
Photography © 2008 by Lars Ranek
Edited text, design, and layout © 2008 by Quadrille Publishing Ltd.

09 10 11 12 13 QRP 10 9 8 7 6 5 4 3 2 1

ISBN-13: 978-0-7407-8094-3
ISBN-10: 0-7407-8094-8

Library of Congress Control Number: 2008935051

www.andrewsmcmeel.com

EDITORIAL DIRECTOR	Anne Furniss
ART DIRECTOR	Helen Lewis
PROJECT EDITOR	Jenni Muir
PHOTOGRAPHER	Lars Ranek
DESIGNER	Vibeke Kaupert
ASSISTANT DESIGNER	Katherine Case
PRODUCTION	Vincent Smith, Marina Asenjo

SCANDINAVIA IS A SMALL CORNER OF THE WORLD. It is inhabited by about 16 million people. Their daily lives are affected importantly by shifting seasons and changing weather patterns. Summer days are long and there is a lot of light, while winter days are cold and very dark.

This has a major impact on people's lives and, of course, on the way we cook. For this book I have tried to portray the contemporary Scandinavian kitchen and mixed it with the way that I personally like to cook. It is based on the seasons, as all good cooking must be, and presented month by month to inspire you to try some recipes from the Scandinavian tradition.

IT IS MY DREAM that people will take the time necessary in their daily lives to sit down and have a nice meal together. The food should be made out of the best, preferably organic, ingredients. It should be prepared with great care and love—without spending a whole day in the kitchen. And when the meal is ready it is an opportunity for us all to sit down together and exchange opinions, share our feelings, and to pass on bits of information on everyday matters. This opportunity should not be missed.

I still strongly believe that you should try to buy as much local produce as you can so that your diet evolves with the seasons. This also gives you something delicious to look forward to, because there is always a new season just around the corner. Summer will bring strawberries, new potatoes, and fresh salad; fall apples, game, and mushrooms; winter cod, oysters, and lobster; and when you just cannot eat any more root vegetables, spring will arrive and it will be time for fresh herbs, rhubarb, and asparagus.

WHEN WRITING A COOKBOOK for people who are probably not familiar with the culinary tradition, methods, and produce of my part of the world, I am faced with the challenge of translating a culture. There are so many things when we cook and eat that are implicit in our culture and that we take completely for granted. Even if we have never cooked or baked according to any specific recipe, we tend to know how our national dishes are made and how they should taste, because they have been passed down through the generations. Food is one of the best ways to exchange cultures without looking at politics or other divergences. Differences in food and cooking are less easily lost in translation. We can just meet as peoples and share some of the gifts this planet has given us: wonderful food, and a tradition of cultivating it in an infinite number of ways depending on our situation in life.

IF I THINK ABOUT SOME OF THE BEST MOMENTS OF MY LIFE, they usually involve sitting around a large table with friends and family, enjoying wonderful food and a nice glass of wine or beer, and talking of something important. I hope to have translated some of these moments into this book and tempted you to do the same—that is, to venture out into the Scandinavian kitchen and make it part of your everyday cooking.

Enjoy.

Trina Hahnemann

January

In winter it is dark for most of the day. The sky

is so low that it seems as though you could reach

out and touch it. Daylight disappears so quickly that

on some days you do not even notice whether it

was there. Breakfast seems to take on a new

significance at this time of year.

Twenty years ago I moved away from Denmark for a while to live in London with my family. We celebrated my son's first birthday in London! In Denmark, it is a tradition to have a big breakfast on your birthday, and parents have to go to the bakery very early, prepare a big breakfast spread, and surprise you. I did not have a baker nearby, so there was only one solution: I had to make the Danish pastries myself. It was not a bad idea, because the pastries turned out beautifully, and it has subsequently become a tradition in our family that I make homemade Danish pastries for everybody's birthday.

Homemade Danish pastries *(Makes 25)*

DOUGH

1 ounce fresh yeast
⅔ cup lukewarm water
1 egg, beaten
1 tablespoon superfine sugar
½ teaspoon salt
2⅓ cups all-purpose flour
1 cup cold butter,
thinly sliced

FILLING

1 vanilla bean
Generous 1 cup light cream
2 egg yolks
2 tablespoons superfine
sugar
1 tablespoon cornstarch

ICING

(optional)
1½ cups confectioners' sugar
3 tablespoons unsweetened
cocoa powder
Hot water

MAKE THE DOUGH. In a mixing bowl, dissolve the yeast in the water. Stir in the egg, superfine sugar, and salt. Add the flour and stir until the dough comes together and leaves the edge of the bowl. Turn it onto a floured counter and knead for 5 minutes until it is shiny but not sticky. Put the dough back in the bowl, cover with plastic wrap, and let rise in the refrigerator for 15 minutes. Roll out the dough into a 20-inch square. Spread the thin slices of butter over the dough about 4 inches in from the edge, so that the square of dough has a smaller square of butter on top. Fold the corners of the dough over the butter to meet in the center, making a square package.

CAREFULLY ROLL THE DOUGH into a 16 by 24-inch rectangle, making sure that it doesn't crack and that the butter stays inside the dough package. Next you want to fold the dough so that the butter becomes layered within it: Fold the bottom third of dough over the middle third, and fold the top third down over that. Roll out the dough again and fold the same way. Put the dough in the refrigerator for 15 minutes, then repeat the rolling and folding process three times, remembering to let the dough rest in the refrigerator for 15 minutes each time.

MAKE THE FILLING. Cut the vanilla bean in half lengthwise and scrape out the seeds with the tip of a knife. Put the vanilla seeds and cream in a pan and bring to a boil. Meanwhile, beat the egg yolks and superfine sugar together until the mixture is pale and fluffy, then stir in the cornstarch. Pour a little bit of the hot cream into the egg mixture to temper it, then pour all of the egg mixture into the pan. Return the pan to a decreased heat and whisk until the custard starts to thicken. Take care not to let the custard boil, and beat continuously in order to avoid scorching. Remove from the heat and let cool before use.

ROLL OUT THE DOUGH to a 20-inch square, then cut it into five rows of 4-inch squares. Place 2 teaspoons of the filling on each square. Take each square's corners and fold them into the middle over the filling, pressing the edges together to seal. Turn each pastry upside down and place them on a baking sheet lined with parchment paper. Cover with a dish towel and let rise for 20 minutes at room temperature. Preheat the oven to 425°F. Brush the pastries with a little beaten egg and bake them for 12 to 15 minutes, or until golden brown. Let cool on a wire rack.

MAKE THE ICING. Mix the confectioners' sugar and cocoa powder together in a bowl, adding a little bit of hot water, and whisk to give a smooth, dark brown paste. Place a spoonful of the icing on each pastry and let set for 10 minutes before serving.

Rye bread is the traditional bread of Scandinavia and varies from region to region. We eat it for lunch and sometimes breakfast. When I was a child, my grandfather would make me a sandwich with a slice of white bread and a slice of rye bread with cheese in the middle. That was my favorite! To make rye bread, you need a sourdough starter, but you only have to make it once if you remember to save a bit of dough before baking for next time. The spelt buns below are my favorite morning buns.

Rye bread *(Makes 1 large loaf)*

SOURDOUGH STARTER
1½ cups rye flour
1¼ cups buttermilk
1 teaspoon coarse sea salt

DOUGH
3 cups lukewarm water
Scant 2¾ cups rye flour
Scant 2¾ cups all-purpose flour
1 tablespoon sea salt

LOAF
1 pound cracked whole rye
Generous 1 cup lukewarm water
2 teaspoons salt

MAKE THE STARTER. Mix the rye flour, buttermilk, and salt in a bowl. Cover with foil and let stand for 3 to 4 days at room temperature (77 to 86°F). And there you have a sourdough starter! But note that if the temperature is too cool, the starter will not develop and instead will go bad.

MAKE THE DOUGH. In a large bowl, dissolve the starter in the lukewarm water. Add the rye flour, all-purpose flour, and salt and stir with a wooden spoon until you have a runny dough. Cover the bowl with a dish towel and set aside for 12 hours at room temperature. I normally do this around dinner time so that it can sit overnight, then I can do the next step in the morning.

MAKE THE LOAF. Add the cracked whole rye, lukewarm water, and salt to the dough and stir again with a wooden spoon until the rye grains are evenly distributed. Take 3 tablespoons of the dough, add 2 tablespoons of coarse salt, and save in a container in the refrigerator ready for the next time you make rye bread. It will last there for up to 8 weeks. Remember to do this every time you make rye bread and you will not need to make the starter again.

POUR THE REST OF THE DOUGH into an 11½ by 4-inch nonstick loaf pan that is 3½ inches deep. (If you do not have a nonstick loaf pan, oil the inside with a little oil.) Cover the pan with a dish towel and let the bread rise for 3 to 6 hours, or until it has reached the rim of the pan. Preheat the oven to 325°F and bake the loaf for 1 hour and 45 minutes. Immediately remove it from the pan and let it cool on a wire rack.

Spelt buns *(Makes 20)*

2 ounces fresh yeast
1¾ cups lukewarm water
1¾ cups yogurt
¼ cup honey
1¾ pounds spelt flour
1 tablespoon salt
1 egg, beaten
Poppy seeds, for sprinkling

DISSOLVE THE YEAST IN THE WATER, then add the yogurt and honey. Sift the spelt flour and salt together and stir thoroughly into the yeast mixture. Let stand for about 5 minutes.

TURN THE DOUGH OUT ONTO A FLOURED COUNTER and knead well. Return the dough to the bowl, cover with a dish towel, and let rise for 1 hour at room temperature.

PREHEAT THE OVEN to 400°F. Dust your hands with some flour and shape the dough into 20 small buns (the dough will be a bit sticky). Put the buns on baking sheets lined with parchment paper. Lightly glaze the buns with the beaten egg and sprinkle with poppy seeds. Bake for 30 minutes, or until golden brown and crispy. Let cool on a wire rack.

Smørrebrød are open-faced sandwiches made with rye bread, and preferably served with aquavit and beer. In the old days people ate very simple ones, such as rye bread with a slice of cold meat, and took them to work as a packed lunch. In the early twentieth century, decorated smørrebrød became fashionable as a late dinner, after theater, or in dance clubs where the guests did not want to spend hours sitting down to a meal and instead wanted to spend their time dancing. Smørrebrød are delicious and luxurious but do not take a lot of time to eat.

Smørrebrød: open-faced sandwiches with flounder, shrimp, and basil dressing *(Serves 4)*

20 fresh basil leaves, finely shredded
3 fresh parsley sprigs, leaves only, minced
1 tablespoon lime juice
¾ cup crème fraîche or sour cream
Salt and pepper
¼ cup rye flour
4 large flounder fillets
Butter, for cooking
4 slices rye bread
4 ounces mixed greens
4 ounces frozen cooked shrimp, defrosted
1 lime, cut into 4 wedges

COMBINE THE BASIL, PARSLEY, AND LIME JUICE in a bowl, then fold in the crème fraîche. Season with salt and pepper and place in the refrigerator.

MIX THE RYE FLOUR WITH SOME SALT AND PEPPER and use this mixture to coat the flounder fillets. In a skillet, melt a little butter and cook the fillets for 4 minutes on each side, or until firm to the touch.

PLACE THE SLICES OF RYE BREAD ON A SERVING DISH. Divide the greens among the bread slices then put a warm flounder fillet and some basil cream on each one. Top with the shrimp and a lime wedge. Serve immediately while the fish is still warm. Cold beer is an excellent accompaniment.

Some dishes are best when they are as plain and simple as possible. Whole fish fried in butter and served with lemon and parsley potatoes: That is simple and tasty!

Pan-fried flounder with potatoes in parsley *(Serves 4)*

1¾ pounds fingerling
potatoes
Salt and pepper
4 whole flounder
1 cup all-purpose or rye flour
9 tablespoons butter
¼ cup minced fresh parsley

FOR SERVING
1 lemon, sliced
Dill sprigs

BOIL THE POTATOES IN A LARGE POT of salted water until tender, then drain. Once they are cool enough to handle, peel them.

RINSE THE FISH IN COLD WATER, then coat each one in the flour, patting off the excess. Melt 5 tablespoons of the butter in a skillet and pan-fry the fish for 5 minutes on each side, or until crisp and golden. Keep the cooked fish warm while you cook the remainder.

MELT THE REMAINING BUTTER in a casserole. Add the peeled potatoes and let them sauté a little before adding the parsley. Season with salt and pepper. Serve immediately with the potatoes, sliced lemon, and dill sprigs.

Norwegian smoked salmon is world famous and tastes great, but salmon also tastes fabulous when marinated rather than smoked. The taste becomes light—and in the recipe below it takes on a deep citrus flavor. The fresh salmon needs to marinate for a few days before freezing overnight. If you want to serve only six people at a time, divide the salmon into four batches and freeze them separately. You can use the salmon in hors d'oeuvres or sandwiches, or serve it as a light dinner or an appetizer in a three-course meal.

Marinated salmon *(Serves 20 to 24)*

1 orange
1 lemon
1½ cups superfine sugar
10 ounces sea salt
1 side of salmon, filleted

FOR SERVING
1 orange
1 lemon
Toasted bread
Green salad

IF YOU HAVE A ZESTER, use it to remove the zest from the orange and lemon because it will look fresh and tasty. Alternatively, finely grate the zest from the fruit. Mix the zests with the sugar and salt.

USE TWEEZERS TO REMOVE ANY PIN-BONES FROM THE SALMON FILLET. Spread the zest mixture evenly over the entire surface of the salmon, then wrap it in plastic wrap and refrigerate for 3 days.

AFTER 3 DAYS, TAKE THE SALMON OUT OF THE REFRIGERATOR, remove the plastic wrap, and wipe off the marinade with a paper towel. Wrap the salmon in plastic wrap and freeze it for 12 hours, then take it out of the freezer and defrost it.

PUT THE SALMON ON A BOARD AND CUT IT INTO THIN SLICES with a very sharp knife. The traditional cutting technique starts diagonally at one corner of the salmon, and then works back toward the center of the fillet.

TO SERVE, remove the zest from the remaining orange and lemon and sprinkle it over the salmon. Serve with toasted bread and a green salad.

In the past 10 years it has become fashionable to serve root vegetables, and star chefs use them creatively in their menus. I think they are very important in our daily diet as well. They are healthy and tasty, can be prepared in a thousand ways, and enjoyed at lunch, in a salad, or as a side dish or garnish at dinner.

Chicken with root vegetables *(Serves 6)*

8 cloves garlic, peeled
1 fairly large chicken
Salt and pepper
1 celery root, peeled and cut into medium-size cubes
3 beets, peeled and cut into medium-size cubes
2 carrots, peeled and cut into medium-size cubes
1 small handful fresh thyme
2 tablespoons olive oil

FOR SERVING
Green salad
Fresh bread

PREHEAT THE OVEN to 400°F. Put six of the garlic cloves inside the chicken and sprinkle the outside with salt and pepper. Place the chicken in an ovenproof dish and roast for 40 minutes.

MEANWHILE, MINCE THE REMAINING GARLIC CLOVES and mix with the celery root, beets, carrots, thyme, olive oil, and salt and pepper.

AFTER 40 MINUTES, TAKE THE CHICKEN OUT OF THE OVEN and lift it out of the dish. Spread the vegetables out evenly in the dish, place the chicken back on top, and return to the oven to roast for another 30 minutes, or until the juices run clear and an instant-read thermometer registers 175°F.

WHEN THE CHICKEN IS DONE, CUT IT INTO EIGHT PIECES and serve with the vegetables along with a green salad and bread.

February

Cross-country skiing in Norway is a hushed and beautiful experience. You go on skis into the mountains with a rucksack containing sandwiches and warm tea on your back. You ski long slopes, you do not have to stand in line, and you are never run over. It is only you and the skis. Everything is so quiet, you can just focus and let your skis cut through the snow. It is hard work and perfect exercise, and when you come home the afternoon sauna or a long hot bath awaits. And hopefully some lovely food.

The northern tip of Denmark is a magnificent place. The light is very special due to the sea's reflections of the sky, which make the light seem to come from all corners of the world. The mountains of southern Norway shelter the sky over Skagen and somehow cleanse the air. Huge sand dunes line the coast in the form of a large arrow pointing north. Two different seas, coming from east and west respectively, meet at the tip, where the currents clash, divide, and return again in an eternal battle, leaving a long sand bar in between that keeps shifting position. Artists have been drawn to Skagen from all over Scandinavia for generations. Many dishes have therefore developed in this area and this is one of its famous fish soups.

Skagen fish soup *(Serves 4)*

FISH STOCK

2 pounds fish bones, from flatfish
1 clove garlic, peeled
1 onion
1 leek
1 carrot
1 large ripe tomato
2 tablespoons olive oil
¾ cup dry white wine
3 bay leaves
10 peppercorns
1 tablespoon salt
8 cups water

SOUP

⅓ cup dry white wine
1 tablespoon lemon juice
¾ cup heavy cream
½ teaspoon saffron strands
1 leek, thinly sliced
1 carrot, diced
½ pound crayfish tails
12 giant shrimp, peeled and deveined
4 ounces salmon fillet
4 ounces pollack fillet
Salt and pepper
Dill sprigs, for garnish

MAKE THE STOCK. Rinse the fish bones in cold water. Coarsely chop the vegetables. In a stockpot, sauté the vegetables in the olive oil for 3 to 5 minutes so that they do not color. Add the white wine, bay leaves, peppercorns, and salt and boil for 5 minutes. Add the fish bones and water. Bring back to a boil, decrease the heat, and simmer for 30 minutes. Pour the stock through a strainer, reserving the liquid and discarding the fish bones and vegetables.

MAKE THE SOUP. Simmer the white wine in a large pot for 5 minutes. Add the reserved fish stock, lemon juice, cream, and saffron and bring slowly to a boil.

ADD THE LEEK, CARROT, CRAYFISH, AND SHRIMP TO THE SOUP. Decrease the heat and let simmer for 5 minutes. Meanwhile, cut the salmon and pollack into ¾-inch cubes. Add the cubed fish and let simmer for another 2 minutes, or until the fish flakes easily and the shrimp is cooked through. Season with salt and pepper, then serve very hot garnished with dill.

PICNIC IN THE SNOW. When you go out for a whole day of cross-country skiing in the mountains, you need to bring a solid lunch that will keep you energized and warm. Spinach soup (you can use frozen spinach if you cannot buy it fresh) and smoked salmon and avocado sandwiches are perfect. Pack the thermos of soup in your basket or rucksack along with your sandwiches and some paper cups and spoons. Enjoy them together in the cold, white mountains.

Spinach soup *(Serves 4)*

2 pounds fresh spinach
2 tablespoons olive oil
1 onion, coarsely chopped
2 cloves garlic,
coarsely chopped
2 large potatoes, peeled
and cubed
4 cups water
½ teaspoon freshly ground
mace
Salt and pepper
⅓ cup heavy cream

REMOVE ANY TOUGH STEMS FROM THE SPINACH LEAVES and rinse them three or four times in cold water. Drain and set aside in a colander. Heat the olive oil in a large pot and sauté the onion and garlic. Stir in the potatoes and 2 cups of the water. Bring to a boil, then decrease the heat and simmer for 15 minutes.

ADD THE SPINACH, MACE, SALT, PEPPER, and the remaining water to the pan. Return to a boil, then decrease the heat, cover, and simmer for 10 minutes. Add the cream and heat through. Blend the soup (using an immersion blender is the easiest way to do it) and adjust the salt and pepper to taste. Store the hot soup in a thermos to take on the picnic.

Smoked salmon sandwiches *(Serves 4)*

SANDWICH SPREAD
3 tablespoons homemade
mayonnaise (page 92)
2 tablespoons yogurt
1 teaspoon Djion mustard
1 teaspoon grated
lemon zest
Salt and pepper

SANDWICHES
8 slices bread, 4 rolls, or
4 pieces rye focaccia
(see Salmon Burgers, page
76), split horizontally
7 ounces mixed greens
12 slices smoked salmon
2 tomatoes, sliced
1 avocado, sliced

MAKE THE SANDWICH SPREAD. In a bowl, mix together the mayonnaise, yogurt, mustard, and zest, adding salt and pepper to taste.

MAKE THE SANDWICHES. On half the bread slices, or the bottoms of the rolls or focaccia pieces, spread the sandwich spread. Divide the greens among the bread and layer with the smoked salmon, tomato, and avocado. Top with the remaining slices of bread, cut in half if desired, and wrap each sandwich in plastic wrap, to pack for the picnic.

Lumpfish roe, which is crisp and has a salty taste like a salty winter sea, is eaten raw, rinsed only in cold water. Usually it is served with blinis or toast, but I love it with crisp potato cakes.

Potato cakes with lumpfish roe and beet salad *(Serves 6)*

BEET SALAD

2 (1-pound) beets

Juice of 1 lime

Salt and pepper

POTATO CAKES

1⅓ pound potatoes, peeled and shredded

4 green onions, minced

4 eggs

¼ cup oatmeal

1 tablespoon sesame seeds

1 tablespoon fresh thyme leaves

1 teaspoon grated nutmeg

2 tablespoons olive oil

FOR SERVING

2 tablespoons minced chives

⅔ cup reduced fat sour cream

14 ounces lumpfish roe, rinsed

MAKE THE BEET SALAD. Preheat the oven to 350°F. Put the beets on a baking sheet and bake for 30 minutes. Let cool slightly. Peel them and cut into very small cubes. Toss with the lime juice, salt, and pepper.

MEANWHILE, MAKE THE POTATO CAKES. In a mixing bowl, combine the shredded potatoes, green onions, eggs, oatmeal, sesame seeds, thyme, nutmeg, and salt and pepper.

HEAT THE OIL IN A SKILLET over medium heat. Use a small spoon to form the potato mixture into small cakes and place them in the oil, pressing down lightly so they are flat. Pan-fry on each side for 5 minutes, or until crisp.

PUT THE POTATO CAKES ON A SERVING DISH. Stir the minced chives into the sour cream. Top each of the cakes with 1 tablespoon of the lumpfish roe, ½ tablespoon of the beet salad, and some of the chive cream. Lastly, grind some pepper over the top and serve immediately with aquavit and beer.

When I was a little girl, I would often spend New Year's Eve with my grandfather on Ærø, an island in the south of Denmark. My aunt would be the hostess on New Year's Eve and cook the dinner. As always, it was cod with mustard sauce and all these lovely condiments. I loved that dinner: the whole atmosphere, the quietness, and the lovely light taste of the cod contrasting with the strong mustard sauce. Then, just after midnight, I would walk home with my grandfather in the new-fallen, squeaking snow. Some suppers can tell stories.

Cod with mustard sauce and condiments *(Serves 6 to 8)*

1 whole cod, rinsed
Salt and pepper
2 pounds fingerling potatoes
8 eggs
7 ounces bacon, diced
10 ounces Pickled Beets
with Star Anise
(page 148), diced

MUSTARD SAUCE
2 tablespoons butter
2 tablespoons all-purpose
flour
⅓ cup heavy cream
¼ cup whole grain mustard

PUT THE WHOLE COD IN A LARGE POT with some salt and pepper. Add enough water to half cover the cod. Cover and bring it to a boil, then decrease the heat and let simmer slowly for 20 minutes, or until the fish flakes easily. Keep the fish warm in the pot with the lid on.

BOIL THE FINGERLING POTATOES IN A LARGE POT of salted water until tender. Drain and keep warm. Boil the eggs for 8 to 10 minutes, until hard, then peel them and cut each one in half. Pan-fry the diced bacon until crisp.

MAKE THE SAUCE. Melt the butter in a small pan over low heat, then add the flour and stir until it forms a smooth paste that comes away from the sides of the pan. Strain 1¾ cups of the cooking liquid from the cod, then add gradually to the pan, stirring well after each addition so that no lumps form as the sauce thickens. Add the cream and mustard and stir again until the sauce is smooth and just coming to a boil. Season with salt and pepper and remove from the heat.

LIFT THE COD OUT OF THE POT and place on a serving dish so it is ready to carve at the table. Put the potatoes, eggs, bacon, beet, and mustard sauce in dishes ready for people to add to their plates as desired.

The quality of Scandinavian lamb is high. Our sheep live on hillsides, meadows, or marshes—all places where the winter weather in particular can be rather rough, with high winds, rain, and even snow. The lambs are exercised as they move around, following the low ebb and the high tide, and so their meat is very tender. This stew is especially nice when the weather is wet and chilly.

Lamb stew with rosemary mashed potatoes *(Serves 6)*

2 tablespoons olive oil
2 pounds lamb shoulder, cut into even-size chunks
2 cloves garlic, chopped
2 rosemary sprigs
10 fresh sage leaves
1¼ cups white wine
¾ cup water
10 ounces Jerusalem artichokes, peeled and cubed
2 leeks, thickly sliced
2 apples, cored and cubed
Salt and pepper

MASHED POTATOES
2 pounds potatoes, peeled and cut into large cubes
2 cloves garlic, peeled
2 rosemary sprigs
1 tablespoon peppercorns
1 tablespoon coarse salt
4 tablespoons butter

IN A SAUTÉ PAN, HEAT THE OIL AND COOK THE MEAT until lightly colored. Add the garlic, rosemary, and sage, then pour in the wine and water and let the meat simmer for 45 minutes, or until tender.

MEANWHILE, MAKE THE MASHED POTATOES. Put the potatoes in a saucepan with the garlic, rosemary, peppercorns, and salt. Add enough water to cover the potatoes, cover, and bring to a boil. Decrease the heat and simmer for 20 minutes, or until tender. Drain, reserving the liquid for later. Discard the rosemary stems.

RETURN THE POTATOES TO THE PAN AND ADD THE BUTTER. Use a balloon whisk to mash the potatoes, leaving the mixture lumpy. If the mash is too heavy, add ¼–¾ cup of the reserved cooking water. Put the pan back over the heat for a couple of minutes and stir with a wooden spoon.

TO FINISH THE STEW, add the Jerusalem artichokes and simmer for 10 minutes, then add the leeks and apples and simmer for 5 minutes more, or until tender. Season with salt and pepper and serve immediately with the potatoes.

A TREAT FOR COLD AFTERNOONS. If life were perfect, we would have more time to drink hot chocolate with our family and friends. One day, during a long and busy spell of hard work, I decided to arrive home early, bake buns, and make hot chocolate for my children as a surprise. It was an especially nasty day outside: snowing, cold, and windy. I got home, made everything ready, lit the candles, and sat down and waited … and waited. Nobody came home that afternoon. They were all busy with their lives on the very day I had decided to do something different with mine. The buns and cocoa were reheated later that night and still tasted wonderful.

Cardamom buns *(Makes 28)*

2 ounces fresh yeast
3 cups lukewarm milk
4 tablespoons butter, melted and left to cool a little
2 pounds all-purpose flour
2 tablespoons superfine sugar
2 teaspoons salt
1 teaspoon ground cardamom
1 egg, beaten

DISSOLVE THE YEAST IN THE LUKEWARM MILK in a mixing bowl, then add the melted butter. Sift the flour, sugar, salt, and cardamom together and stir the dry ingredients into the milk mixture. When a dough has formed that comes cleanly from the edges of the bowl, turn it out onto a floured counter and knead for 5 minutes.

RETURN THE DOUGH TO THE BOWL, cover with a dish towel, and let rise in a warm place for 1 hour. Turn the dough out onto the counter and knead again. Shape into 28 small buns. Place them on two baking sheets lined with parchment paper. Cover with dish towels and let rise again for 20 minutes.

PREHEAT THE OVEN to 400°F. Lightly glaze each bun with beaten egg. Bake for 20 to 25 minutes, or until golden brown. Make the hot chocolate while the cardamom buns are in the oven. Serve the freshly baked buns with butter on the side.

Hot chocolate *(Serves 4)*

9 ounces good-quality semisweet chocolate
4 cups whole milk
1 teaspoon superfine sugar
¾ cup heavy cream

MELT THE CHOCOLATE VERY GENTLY in a small, heavy pan, then add a little bit of the milk and stir until smooth. Repeat until half of the milk is used, then add the sugar. Stir in the rest of the milk.

BRING THE HOT CHOCOLATE TO JUST UNDER BOILING POINT, stirring constantly so that it does not burn. Turn the heat off. Whip the cream until it forms soft peaks. (If you are not serving the hot chocolate immediately, keep the cream cold until you are ready to use it.)

SERVE THE HOT CHOCOLATE with spoonfuls of the cold whipped cream on top. Serve with freshly baked cardamom buns and butter.

March

This time of year is neither winter nor spring. In March you long for spring to arrive while the

winter stubbornly refuses to retire. The gloominess of the month can be quite beautiful and puts

you in a melancholy, reflective mood. Food is one of the best ways to comfort yourself. Mussels

are perfect at this time, also soups and warm stews. Most importantly: a kartoffelkage will raise

the spirits and make you appreciate any gloomy March day.

In Scandinavia, this is the best and cheapest dish ever. We have lots of mussels in the seas around Scandinavia—the blue ones are most common and there are plenty of them. They are easy to prepare and cost almost nothing, so they are the perfect thing to cook on a cold, romantic winter's night when you dream of early spring.

Mussels steamed in wine, vegetables, and parsley *(Serves 2)*

2 pounds mussels
1 tablespoon olive oil
2 cloves garlic, chopped
1 carrot, cut into thin strips
1 leek, cut into thin strips
¾ cup white wine
10 thyme sprigs
Salt and pepper
¾ cup heavy cream
6 tablespoons chopped fresh flat-leaf parsley

SCRUB THE MUSSELS thoroughly and tug out any beards that may be hanging from the shells. Discard any broken or open mussels or those that refuse to close when the shells are tapped. Rinse the mussels in cold water a couple of times.

IN A LARGE PAN, HEAT THE OIL and slowly cook the garlic for a couple of minutes. Add the mussels, carrot, leek, wine, thyme, and salt and pepper. Stir gently, cover, and simmer for 5 minutes.

ADD THE CREAM and parsley and simmer for another 2 minutes. Discard any mussels that have not opened. Season with salt and pepper and serve immediately with a lovely loaf of bread and a nice bottle of wine.

Another tradition at this time of year is to eat fish roe. You can buy a lot of different roe products in Scandinavia. Sweden's supermarkets have a huge selection of pastes in tubes: they are very salty and you eat them on bread for breakfast and lunch. I prefer freshly boiled cod roe, sliced and served on a piece of rye bread with a creamy herb dressing.

Smørrebrød: cod roe on rye bread *(Serves 4)*

1 pound cod roe
1 tablespoon sea salt
4 slices rye bread
Butter, for spreading
Dill sprigs, for garnish

DRESSING
2 tablespoons crème fraîche or sour cream
2 tablespoons homemade mayonnaise (page 92)
1 tablespoon lemon juice
1 tablespoon chopped fresh dill
1 tablespoon chopped chives
Sea salt and pepper

PUT THE COD ROE IN A POT with a generous quantity of water and the sea salt. Boil for 30 minutes, or until they turn opaque and golden, and rise to the surface of the water. Remove the roe with a slotted spoon and let cool.

MEANWHILE, MAKE THE DRESSING. In a small bowl combine the crème fraîche, mayonnaise, lemon juice, dill, and chives and season with salt and pepper.

WHEN THE COD ROE HAS COOLED, CUT IT INTO SLICES. Spread the rye bread with butter and arrange on four plates. Put four or five slices of cod roe on each piece of bread. Top with a tablespoon of the herb dressing and garnish with dill. Serve for lunch with cold beer.

In March the sea is very cold and the lakes and rivers in the northern part of Scandinavia are frozen solid. Nevertheless, many people take a swim at this time of year—it is very healthy and some people believe that it prolongs life. Right after you come out of the cold water, you go into the sauna. Later on you deserve a nice bowl of tasty, hot soup—there is nothing like it on a cold winter's night.

Yogurt and wheat berry bread *(Makes 2 loaves)*

7 ounces wheat berries
2 cups water, plus extra for glazing
1¾ cups low-fat yogurt
2 ounces fresh yeast
3 tablespoons vegetable oil
2 teaspoons salt
1 teaspoon superfine sugar
Scant 3 cups spelt flour
Scant 3 cups all-purpose flour, plus extra for dusting

PUT THE WHEAT BERRIES IN A PAN with the water and bring to a boil. Decrease the heat and let simmer, uncovered, for 15 minutes. Remove the pan from the heat, pour the contents into a mixing bowl, and let cool a little.

MIX IN THE YOGURT. Add the yeast and stir until it has dissolved. Stir in the oil, salt, and sugar. Lastly add the two flours and keep stirring until the dough leaves the sides of the bowl.

TURN THE DOUGH OUT onto a floured counter and knead for 10 minutes. Put the dough back in the bowl, cover with a dish towel, and set aside to rise for 1 hour at room temperature.

AFTER IT HAS RISEN, DIVIDE THE DOUGH IN TWO, knead very lightly, and shape into 2 round loaves. Place each one on a baking sheet lined with parchment paper. Let rise again for 20 minutes.

PREHEAT THE OVEN to 400°F. Glaze the loaves with some extra water before they go into the oven. Bake for 45 minutes. The bread is done when you knock on the base of each loaf and it sounds hollow. Let cool on a wire rack.

Jerusalem artichoke soup *(Serves 4)*

2 pounds Jerusalem artichokes, cubed
1 leek, sliced
2 cloves garlic, chopped
2 teaspoons salt
4 cups water
1 beet
⅓ cup light cream
Salt and pepper
2 cups vegetable oil

PUT THE JERUSALEM ARTICHOKES in a medium pot with the leek, garlic, salt, and water. Bring to a boil, then decrease the heat and simmer for 15 minutes. Meanwhile, peel the beet, then use a vegetable peeler to cut it into long ribbons. Set aside to drain on a paper towel.

PUREE THE SOUP IN A BLENDER or food processor until smooth, then return to the pot. Add the cream and bring to a boil, stirring constantly. Remove from the heat, season with salt and pepper and keep warm.

HEAT THE VEGETABLE OIL IN A SAUTÉ PAN and fry the beet ribbons for a few minutes. Remove from the oil with a slotted spoon and let drain on paper towels.

SERVE THE SOUP HOT, garnished with the beet ribbons.

There are many different kinds of oysters in Scandinavia. My favorites are from Limfjorden, a bay in northern Jutland. The shells are circular, and the oysters are big and very meaty. It is a shame to eat them any way but plain, but if you insist on some kind of sauce, serve them with this red onion vinaigrette.

Oysters *(Serves 4)*

¼ cup red wine vinegar
2 tablespoons superfine sugar
1 small red onion, very finely minced
24 oysters
Lemon wedges, for serving

WHISK THE RED WINE VINEGAR with the sugar until the sugar has dissolved. Mix the red onion into the vinegar and set aside.

OPEN EACH OYSTER WITH AN OYSTER KNIFE and release the meat from the bottom shell so they are easy to eat at the table. Serve the oysters with the red onion vinaigrette and lemon wedges.

Captain's stew is made of potatoes and meat with bay leaves and lots of black pepper. This is one of my favorite winter dishes. I do not prepare it often, only a couple of times each winter. It's solid and tasty and will fill you up for quite some time.

Captain's stew *(Serves 6)*

¼ cup olive oil
2 pounds chuck steak, cut into even-size chunks
6 cups water
4 pounds potatoes, peeled and diced
1 onion, minced
4 bay leaves
1 tablespoon peppercorns
1 tablespoon sea salt
4 tablespoons butter
Salt and pepper

FOR SERVING
Chopped chives
Whole grain mustard
Sliced rye bread
Pickled Beets with Star Anise (page 148)

HEAT THE OIL IN A LARGE SAUCEPAN and, when medium-hot, add the steak and cook until lightly colored. Add the water and bring gradually to a boil, skimming any froth from the surface (it takes about 5 minutes to catch it all).

ADD THE POTATOES, ONION, BAY LEAVES, PEPPERCORNS, AND SALT. Simmer for 1½ hours, or until the meat is very tender and falls apart easily—you may need to cook it for another 30 minutes or so.

STIR IN THE BUTTER. Use a balloon whisk to mash the potatoes and meat together—though note that the stew should remain lumpy. Season with salt and pepper. Discard the bay leaves.

TO SERVE, SPOON THE STEW INTO BOWLS AND SPRINKLE WITH CHIVES. Accompany with whole grain mustard, slices of rye bread, and pickled beets.

Biff Lindström, a slightly spicy meat patty sweetened with beets, is best as a Sunday lunch or as a hangover cure after a long night out. It is sometimes served with a fried egg on top. This is my Swedish version, but there are many variations. In Denmark, bøf tartar is a dish of raw meat with all the condiments and an egg yolk on top. I'm not a fan of raw meat (I like raw fish better) and therefore prefer biff Lindström to bøf tartar.

Biff Lindström *(Serves 4)*

1 onion, minced
2 tablespoons capers, minced
2 tablespoons Pickled Beets with Star Anise (page 148), minced
2 tablespoons minced chives
1 pound ground beef
4 egg yolks
1 tablespoon Worcestershire sauce
Salt and pepper
Olive oil, for cooking

FRIED POTATOES
2 pounds potatoes
3 tablespoons butter
2 tablespoons olive oil

BALSAMICO BEANS
10 ounces green beans
3 tablespoons balsamic vinegar
2 teaspoons superfine sugar

COMBINE THE ONION, CAPERS, BEETS, AND CHIVES in a mixing bowl with the ground beef, egg yolks, Worcestershire sauce, salt, and pepper. Shape into four hamburgers and season on both sides with salt and pepper.

MAKE THE POTATOES. Boil the potatoes in a large pot of salted water until tender, then drain. Once they are cool enough to handle, peel and cut into even-size cubes. Heat the butter and olive oil in a sauté pan and cook the potatoes, turning them regularly, for about 10 minutes or until crisp. Sprinkle with salt and pepper.

MAKE THE BEANS. In a steamer basket, steam the beans for 5 minutes; drain well. In a small pan, stir together the balsamic vinegar and sugar and simmer for 3 minutes. Toss the beans in the balsamic glaze until hot.

MEANWHILE, COOK THE BURGERS in olive oil for 3 to 8 minutes on each side, depending on whether you want them medium or well-done. Serve with the potatoes and balsamico beans on the side.

You can buy these traditional pastries, which look like large potatoes (kartoffel), in most bakeries around Denmark. Choux pastry is covered with cocoa-dusted marzipan and filled with the most luscious cream you can imagine. If you like to bake, then take the time one day to prepare this dessert. I promise: You are not going to regret it.

Kartoffelkage (Makes 8 pastries)

CHOUX PASTRY

6½ tablespoons butter, plus extra for greasing

Generous ¾ cup water

Pinch of salt

¾ cup all-purpose flour

2 to 3 eggs, beaten

CREAM

1 vanilla bean

Generous 1 cup light cream

3 egg yolks

3 tablespoons superfine sugar

1 tablespoon cornstarch

Generous ⅓ cup heavy cream

MARZIPAN TOPPING

14 ounces ready-rolled marzipan

Generous 1 cup unsweetened cocoa powder

MAKE THE PASTRY. Combine the butter and water in a pot over low heat and let the butter melt. Turn up the heat and bring to a boil.

SIFT THE SALT WITH THE FLOUR. Turn off the heat under the pot, add the flour to the liquid, and stir with a wooden spoon until a firm, smooth paste is formed. Beat the paste until it comes away from the edge of the pot in a ball. Let cool for about 10 minutes. Add the beaten eggs little by little, beating well each time. Continue adding egg until the mixture is smooth and glossy. Sometimes you need to use all the beaten eggs, sometimes not, so it is fine if a little is left over.

PUT THE DOUGH IN A PASTRY BAG with a ¼-inch plain tip. Lightly butter a sheet of parchment paper and place on a baking sheet. On one side of the paper, pipe a 2½-inch line of choux pastry. Follow with a second line parallel to the first one, so that they cling together. Pipe a third line on top of the other two. Repeat to make eight of these choux buns.

PREHEAT THE OVEN to 400°F. Bake the buns for 20 to 30 minutes. Do not open the oven door before the choux has set or the pastry may not rise. The pastries are done when they are golden brown and firm. Place them on a wire rack. Cut a small hole in the side of each bun to let the steam out, so the pastry will not go soft inside. Let cool.

MAKE THE CREAM. Cut the vanilla bean in half lengthwise and scrape out the seeds with the tip of a knife. Combine the vanilla seeds with the light cream in a pot and heat until steaming hot. Meanwhile, whisk the egg yolks and sugar together in a mixing bowl until the mixture turns pale and fluffy, then whisk in the cornstarch. Stir one-third of the hot cream into the egg mixture, then pour the egg mixture into the pot. Stir over low heat until it starts to thicken. Remove from the heat and let cool. When the cream filling is cold, whip the heavy cream until it forms stiff peaks and fold it in.

MAKE THE TOPPING AND ASSEMBLE THE PASTRIES. Split each choux bun in half horizontally and place a couple of spoonfuls of cream filling on the bottom half. Place the other half on top, being careful not to press them together. Take the marzipan and cut it into eight oval shapes about 3 inches long, using an oval pastry cutter or a small, sharp knife. Lay the marzipan ovals on a piece of parchment paper and dust them with cocoa until they are completely covered. Carefully lay one over each cream-filled pastry.

PLACE THE FILLED PASTRIES ON A SERVING DISH and keep cool until serving time. I prefer them served with good coffee or espresso—the bitterness of the coffee goes well the luscious pastries.

April

Copenhagen bursts into life in early spring. Everybody comes out of their houses or apartments, the cafés put tables and chairs on the sidewalk, all the small beautiful squares become populated again, and there are lots of cultural events and festivals. It's a great time to sit outside, lunching on herrings and drinking the famous beer and aquavit.

Herring live in the chilly waters that surround the Scandinavian coast. Some people have them for lunch daily; they are an important part of meals at special occasions such as Easter, too. Offer three or four different kinds of herrings at one meal and serve them on rye bread with sliced raw onion and dill on top.

Marinated fried herring *(Serves 4)*

BRINE

2 cups distilled vinegar

1½ cups superfine sugar

1 tablespoon peppercorns

4 bay leaves

MAKE THE BRINE. In a saucepan, combine the vinegar, sugar, peppercorns, and bay leaves and bring to a boil. Reduce the heat and simmer for 30 minutes. Remove from the heat and set aside to cool.

HERRING

12 fresh herring fillets

¼ cup Dijon mustard

1 bunch dill, chopped

1½ cups rye flour

6½ tablespoons butter

2 onions, sliced

MAKE THE HERRING. Cut off the little fin on the back side of each fillet. In a small bowl, mix the mustard and dill together. Spread out the rye flour on a tray or large plate.

PLACE THE HERRING FILLETS SKIN-SIDE DOWN in the flour, pressing them down a bit so that the flour sticks to them. Spread 1 teaspoon of the mustard mixture over each herring and fold them over so that the fillets form a square sandwich. Make sure the skin is covered in flour.

HEAT THE BUTTER in a skillet and cook the herring until firm to the touch, 3 to 5 minutes on each side depending on size.

PLACE THE COOKED HERRING in a large plastic container, laying them side by side. Scatter the sliced onions over the herring, then cover with the brine. Marinate for 2 hours, or overnight in the refrigerator. They will keep for up to a week in the refrigerator.

Homemade white herring *(Serves 12)*

12 salted herring fillets

1 red onion, sliced

2 carrots, thinly sliced

2 dill sprigs, fronds picked off

COVER THE SALTED HERRING FILLETS with cold water and let soak for 6 hours.

MAKE THE BRINE. Combine the vinegar, water, sugar, peppercorns, mustard seeds, coriander seeds, allspice, cloves, and bay leaves in a pot and bring to a boil. Reduce the heat and simmer for 30 minutes. Set aside to cool.

BRINE

1¾ cups vinegar

1¾ cups water

1¼ cups superfine sugar

2 tablespoons peppercorns

2 tablespoons mustard seeds

1 tablespoon coriander seeds

15 allspice berries

10 whole cloves

2 bay leaves

DRAIN THE HERRING FILLETS and cut into 1¼-inch slices. Place in a sterilized preserving jar with the sliced onion, carrots, and dill fronds. Pour over the cold brine, seal tightly, and refrigerate for a week before serving. Then simply remove the pieces of herring and any parts of the brine as desired. Stored in the refrigerator, the herrings will last for up to 3 months.

Smoked salmon used to be something special that you would eat only at dinner parties or on special occasions, but this has changed as prices have come down. If you buy a whole side of smoked salmon, you can cut it into three or four pieces and freeze them separately. Freshly cut smoked salmon tastes far better than precut slices, so try to do it yourself.

Smoked salmon and horseradish cream with crunchy cucumber and caraway seed salad *(Serves 4)*

10 ounces mixed greens
1 cucumber
1 tablespoon caraway seeds
12 slices smoked salmon

DRESSING
1¼ cups reduced fat sour cream
2 tablespoons grated fresh horseradish, or prepared horseradish
½ teaspoon sugar
1 tablespoon lemon juice
Salt and pepper

TEAR THE GREENS into small pieces. Cut the cucumber in half lengthwise and then cut it into thin slices. Mix the greens, cucumber, and caraway seeds in a salad bowl.

MAKE THE DRESSING. Mix the sour cream, horseradish, and sugar together, stirring very gently. Add the lemon juice and season with salt and pepper.

ADD HALF THE DRESSING TO THE SALAD AND TOSS. Arrange the smoked salmon on plates with the dressed salad on the side. Pass the remaining dressing at the table. Serve with nice homebaked bread, such as Caraway Seed Bread (page 92) or Yogurt and Wheat Berry Bread (page 48).

Smørrebrød (open-faced sandwiches) are traditionally served at lunchtime, though I also like to eat them for supper on Sunday. This is the perfect meal to serve guests staying for the weekend, in which case I prepare them with other smørrebrød, such as those on pages 14, 44, and 118. If you can't find lovage, use tarragon or parsley.

Smørrebrød: chicken and lovage salad on rye bread *(Serves 4)*

1 bunch lovage
1 small chicken
1 tablespoon sea salt
1 tablespoon peppercorns
2 tablespoons reduced fat sour cream
2 tablespoons homemade mayonnaise (page 92)
Salt and pepper

FOR SERVING
4 slices rye bread
Crisp lettuce leaves

PICK THE LEAVES from four stems of the lovage and set them aside for the salad. Put the chicken in a pot with the four bare lovage stems, salt, and peppercorns. Add enough water to cover the chicken. Bring to a boil, then reduce the heat and simmer for 1 hour, or until the meat is white.

WHEN THE CHICKEN IS COOKED, carefully lift it out of the water and place on a tray. Once it is cool enough to handle, remove the skin and pick the meat from the bones. Discard the bones and skin.

CHOP THE RESERVED LOVAGE LEAVES. Put the chicken pieces in a mixing bowl with 6 tablespoons of the chopped lovage, plus the sour cream and mayonnaise. Fold together and season with salt and pepper.

ARRANGE THE SLICES OF RYE BREAD ON FOUR PLATES, then place the lettuce on the bread and add the chicken salad. Take the remaining lovage stems and cut them in two lengthwise. Use them to garnish the smørrebrød before serving.

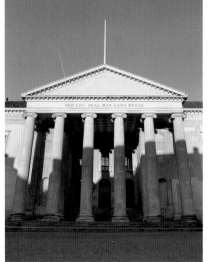

Lamb rib roast is the cut of lamb that is most tasty. It should not be roasted for so long that the meat is no longer pink. When making this dish, ask the butcher to take out all the bones from the roast for you. Mint and lamb are meant for each other, because the flavor of lamb is enhanced by the freshness of the mint.

Mint, apricot, and celery stuffed lamb with spinach and minted roast potatoes *(Serves 8)*

2 celery stalks, coarsely chopped
½ cup dried apricots, coarsely chopped
2 cloves garlic, coarsely chopped
30 fresh mint leaves
4 pounds lamb rib roast, boned
Salt and pepper

POTATOES
2 pounds new potatoes, halved
3 mint sprigs
¼ cup olive oil

SPINACH
6½ pounds spinach leaves
4 tablespoons butter
½ teaspoon nutmeg

PREHEAT THE OVEN to 400°F. Mix the celery, apricots, and garlic with the mint leaves.

LAY THE LAMB OUT ON A CUTTING BOARD. Rub the top with salt and pepper and spread the mint-apricot mixture over the surface. Fold it so that the two sides meet.

TAKE SOME KITCHEN STRING and tie it around the lamb at even intervals. Place the lamb in a roasting pan and sprinkle with salt and pepper. Roast for 1 hour and 20 minutes, or until an instant-read thermometer registers 140°F (for medium) or 175°F (for well done).

MAKE THE POTATOES. Place the potatoes and one of the mint sprigs in a large pan of salted water and boil until the potatoes are tender. Drain well.

PICK THE LEAVES from the remaining mint sprigs. Heat the olive oil in a sauté pan and sauté the cooked potatoes with the mint leaves until crispy. Season with salt and pepper.

MAKE THE SPINACH. Remove any tough stems from the spinach leaves and rinse them three or four times in cold water. Drain.

MELT THE BUTTER in a large sauté pan. Add the spinach, nutmeg, salt, and pepper and cook, stirring constantly, until the spinach wilts. Take it off the heat immediately, being careful not to overcook—spinach is at its nicest when still green and fairly toothsome.

CARVE THE ROAST LAMB into slices and serve immediately with the spinach and potatoes.

Some desserts survive for generations. This one was very popular in the 1950s when there were real housewives who had the time to cook all day long, and everything was spick and span when the husband came home. I can't say that's the way it is today—in my household or in Scandinavian households in general.

Lemon mousse *(Serves 8)*

1 tablespoon
granulated gelatin
3 eggs, separated
⅓ cup superfine sugar
Generous ⅓ cup heavy cream
Juice of 3 lemons
1 teaspoon finely grated
lemon zest

FOR SERVING
⅓ cup heavy cream
Candied Lemon Zest
(see below)

SOAK THE GELATIN GRANULES IN A HEATPROOF BOWL OF COLD WATER for about 5 minutes. In a mixing bowl, beat the egg yolks and sugar together with an electric mixer until pale and fluffy. In another large mixing bowl, whisk the egg whites until stiff peaks form. In a separate bowl, whip the heavy cream until soft peaks form.

PLACE THE BOWL WITH THE SOFTENED GELATIN GRANULES OVER A PAN OF HOT WATER and dissolve the granules gently. Turn off the heat, pour in the lemon juice, and add the zest. Slowly pour the gelatin mixture into the egg yolk mixture, stirring all the time. Set aside in a cool place until the mousse is starting to set.

FOLD THE EGG WHITES AND THE WHIPPED CREAM into the gelatin mixture. Pour into one large serving dish or several small dishes and chill for a couple of hours in the refrigerator.

TO SERVE, whip the heavy cream until it forms stiff peaks, then serve the mousse with the cream and candied lemon zest.

Candied lemon zest

1 lemon
⅓ cup superfine sugar
¼ cup water

CUT THE ZEST FROM THE LEMON IN LONG, THIN STRIPS using a zester, then squeeze the juice from the fruit. Combine the zest, juice, sugar, and water in a small pan and bring to a boil. Reduce the heat and simmer for 5 minutes.

REMOVE THE PAN FROM THE HEAT. Separate the lemon strips from each other and spread out on a baking sheet. Let cool and dry.

Scandinavia's traditional almond cakes are eaten on special occasions such as New Year's Eve, when they are served at midnight with champagne. At weddings and other festive receptions you have them after dinner with coffee. I serve them all year-round because they are my favorite. I also give them as gifts, nicely wrapped in cellophane bags.

Kransekage: almond cakes *(Makes 24)*

⅔ cup blanched almonds
1 cup superfine sugar
2 egg whites
1 pound Homemade
Marzipan (below)
24 walnut halves
12 dried apricots, cut into 4
strips each
7 ounces good-quality
semisweet chocolate

PROCESS THE ALMONDS AND SUGAR TOGETHER in a food processor until finely ground. Add the egg whites and process until you have a smooth, white mixture. Make sure the mixture does not get too hot in the processor, otherwise the egg whites start clotting.

GRATE THE MARZIPAN and then blend it into the almond mixture. Transfer the mixture to a bowl, cover tightly, and let rest in the refrigerator for a couple of hours or overnight.

SHAPE THE MIXTURE INTO 24 (3½ by ¾-inch) rectangular cakes, like shortbread fingers. Press a walnut half on one end of each almond finger, and two strips of dried apricot on the other end.

PREHEAT THE OVEN to 375°F. Place the shortbread fingers on a baking sheet lined with parchment paper. Bake for 15 to 18 minutes, or until lightly golden brown. Let cool on a wire rack.

MELT THE CHOCOLATE GENTLY in a double boiler, then dip the bottom of each almond cake in the chocolate and set on a piece of parchment paper.

Homemade marzipan *(Makes 1 pounds)*

3⅓ cups blanched almonds
1 cup confectioners' sugar,
plus extra for kneading
¼ cup water

PROCESS THE ALMONDS in the food processor until they become a paste. Add the confectioners' sugar, process again, then add the water and process again until it becomes a firm paste.

TAKE THE MARZIPAN OUT OF THE FOOD PROCESSOR and knead it on a counter dusted with confectioners' sugar. Now it is ready to be used for cakes and candies. It will keep for up to 2 weeks in the refrigerator, and you'll find it tastes much better than the store-bought stuff.

May

Spring is a very beautiful season. Everything becomes green and crisp and starts to burst. This is the time of the year for anybody who is into food. The season means new and fresh vegetables. Nothing is better than a blossoming green backyard. It can be so green that it almost blinds you. There will be fresh herbs, asparagus, cabbage, and rhubarb.

The burger is a fantastic invention. Although it is not Scandinavian, we have taken to it with passion because we love everything that has ground meat and comes with bread. What, then, could be more natural than putting our most famous fish, the salmon, in a burger?

Salmon burgers *(Serves 4)*

RYE FOCACCIA
1 ounce fresh yeast
3 cups cold water
1 tablespoon honey
4 tablespoons olive oil
2 teaspoons salt
3½ cups rye flour
3½ cups all-purpose flour
1 tablespoon coarse sea salt

SALMON BURGERS
1½ pounds salmon fillet
1 green onion, chopped
1 tablespoon capers, chopped
1 egg, beaten
2 tablespoons fresh bread crumbs
Salt and pepper
Olive oil, for cooking

DRESSING
2 tablespoons homemade mayonnaise (page 92)
2 tablespoons minced chives
1 tablespoon crème fraîche
1 teaspoon lemon juice

FOR SERVING
Mixed lettuce leaves
2 tomatoes, sliced
Chopped chives, for garnish

MAKE THE FOCACCIA. Dissolve the yeast in the water. Add the honey, 2 tablespoons of the olive oil, and 2 teaspoons of salt and stir again. Mix in both flours to form a very wet dough, then stir with a wooden spoon for 10 minutes or, if you are using an electric mixer, let it run for 5 minutes. Scrape the dough out into a container, cover, and refrigerate overnight.

PREHEAT THE OVEN to 425°F. Line a 12 by 16-inch baking sheet with parchment paper. Press the dough into the sheet as evenly as possible, then press "dimples" in the surface. Drizzle with the remaining 2 tablespoons olive oil and sprinkle with the coarse sea salt.

BAKE THE FOCACCIA for 10 minutes, then turn the oven down to 400°F and continue baking for another 20 minutes, or until the bread sounds hollow when tapped on the base. Let cool on a wire rack.

MAKE THE BURGERS. Remove the skin from the salmon and use a large knife to chop the flesh until it is finely ground. Put the salmon in a mixing bowl and add the green onion and capers. Fold in the egg, bread crumbs, and salt and pepper.

CAREFULLY SHAPE THE MIXTURE INTO FOUR LARGE PATTIES. Heat the oil in a skillet and cook the patties over medium heat for 4 minutes on each side, or until cooked through. Be careful when turning them as they are very delicate.

MAKE THE DRESSING. In a small bowl, combine the mayonnaise, chives, crème fraîche, and lemon juice and season with salt and pepper.

TO SERVE, cut four slabs from the rye focaccia and halve each one horizontally. Save the rest of the bread for another meal. Spread the dressing over the cut side of each piece of bread, then lay on some lettuce, a salmon burger, sliced tomatoes, and a sprinkling of chives and sandwich with the remaining bread. Serve immediately with cold beer.

Sea trout tastes wonderful hot or cold. The fish lives wild and is also farmed in Norway. Here it is served with all the best of May: new potatoes and the special Danish smoked cheese called rygeost. This is a fresh cows' milk cheese that is smoked in an oven. You can eat it on rye bread or use it for dressings and sauces. Smoked ricotta or other soft smoked cheese would be a good alternative.

Baked trout with new potatoes and smoked-cheese cream *(Serves 6)*

2 carrots, sliced
2 leeks, sliced
¼ cup olive oil
Salt and pepper
1 (4-pound) sea trout
1 lemon, sliced
1 tablespoon peppercorns
2 or 3 flat-leaf parsley sprigs
2 pounds new potatoes
4 ounces rygeost or smoked ricotta
2 tablespons reduced fat sour cream
4 ounces radishes, coarsely chopped
2 tablespoons minced chives

PREHEAT THE OVEN to 400°F. Arrange the carrots and leeks on a large baking sheet and drizzle with the olive oil. Sprinkle with salt and pepper and turn to coat the vegetables with the oil. Lay the trout on top. Add the sliced lemon and scatter with the peppercorns, 1 tablespoon of salt, and the parsley. Cover the sheet with foil and bake for 40 minutes. To check if cooked, lift the flap of the fish; the flesh should be pale pink and firm.

MEANWHILE, BOIL THE POTATOES in a large pot of salted water until tender, then drain and slice.

MIX THE SMOKED CHEESE, sour cream, radishes, and chives together and season with salt and pepper. Gently mix in the potatoes.

SERVE THE TROUT WITH THE POTATO SALAD and roasted vegetables, using the hot lemon slices as a garnish.

Combining different vegetables in all kinds of salads has always been one of the things I love most about cooking. I started preparing salads when I was a child. I was in charge of the cooking once every week. I took everything out of the refrigerator and, without knowing the rules, combined them. Some days it was fantastic—other days did not go so well. But I learned a lot, and one of the most important lessons was: taste.

Baked green and white asparagus salad *(Serves 4)*

15 green asparagus spears
15 white asparagus spears
¼ cup olive oil
Grated zest and juice of 1 lemon
Salt and pepper

PREHEAT THE OVEN to 350°F. Cut 1¼ inches from the base of each asparagus spear, then peel the white ones only from the tips down. Rinse the asparagus with the tips downward in cold water. Place the spears in a baking dish and mix well with the olive oil, lemon zest, juice, and salt and pepper.

BAKE THE SPEARS for 5 to 7 minutes, or until just tender. You can then serve them as they are, hot or cold, or cut the spears into smaller pieces, making sure the lemon zest and juice are still coating the asparagus.

Cauliflower with coarse almonds *(Serves 4)*

1 medium-size head cauliflower
½ cup whole almonds
1 clove garlic, crushed
Juice of 1 lemon
1 tablespoon white wine vinegar
¼ cup olive oil
¼ cup chopped fresh chervil or flat-leaf parsley
Salt and pepper

RINSE AND DRY THE CAULIFLOWER, cut it into very small florets, and place in a bowl.

CHOP THE ALMONDS UNTIL MEDIUM-FINE and mix with the crushed garlic, lemon juice, vinegar, olive oil, and salt and pepper.

MIX THE DRESSING WITH THE CAULIFLOWER and let rest for 30 minutes. Season the salad with salt and pepper, then sprinkle with chervil or parsley before serving.

Carrot salad with parsley and pine nuts *(Serves 4)*

4 carrots
2 tablespoons pine nuts
¼ cup coarsely chopped fresh flat-leaf parsley
2 tablespoons olive oil
Juice of 1 lemon
Salt and pepper

PEEL THE CARROTS and trim the bottoms and tops. Use a vegetable peeler to cut the carrots into ribbons.

IN A DRY SKILLET, TOAST THE PINE NUTS OVER MEDIUM HEAT, stirring constantly, until golden brown.

IN A SALAD BOWL, COMBINE the carrots, pine nuts, parsley, olive oil, and lemon juice. Season with salt and pepper before serving.

Meatballs are a national favorite in many countries and served in many different ways. I grow lots of thyme in my small urban backyard from May until September, so I have it right at hand. Instead of boiling cabbage to serve with the meatballs, I prefer to pan-fry it in butter so that it stays crisp and retains its nutty taste. Cowberries (called lingonberries in the United States) grow in cold areas and are very sour, like cranberries. You therefore need to cook them with a lot of sugar, but I still like to keep the taste quite fresh and sour.

Meatballs with thyme, green cabbage, and lingonsylt *(Serves 4)*

1½ pounds ground veal and pork mixture
1 small onion, minced
3 tablespoons fresh thyme leaves, minced
2 eggs
1½ cups fresh bread crumbs
2 tablespoons all-purpose flour
Generous ⅓ cup sparkling water
Salt and pepper
1½ pounds new potatoes
Olive oil
About 3 tablespoons butter
1 green cabbage, quartered
Cowberry Compote (below)

MIX THE GROUND MEATS, onion, thyme, and eggs together and beat well. Stir in the bread crumbs and flour and beat again. Mix in the sparkling water and season with salt and pepper.

PREHEAT THE OVEN to 350°F. Cut the potatoes in half lengthwise. Place in an ovenproof dish and mix with a little olive oil, salt, and pepper. Bake for 1 hour, or until tender.

MEANWHILE, USE A SPOON AND YOUR FREE HAND TO SHAPE THE MEAT MIXTURE into small round balls. Heat 1 tablespoon of the butter and some olive oil together in a large skillet and cook the meatballs on all sides until golden brown. Transfer the meatballs to a baking dish and bake in the oven for 10 minutes, or until cooked through.

ONCE THE MEATBALLS ARE IN THE OVEN, melt the remaining butter in a large skillet and pan-fry the cabbage in it for a couple of minutes on each side of the wedge. Sprinkle with pepper and serve the cabbage together with the meatballs, potatoes, and cowberry compote.

Cowberry (or cranberry) compote

2 pounds fresh or frozen lingonberries (cowberries) or cranberries
¾ cup water
3 cups superfine sugar

COMBINE THE BERRIES AND WATER IN A SAUCEPAN and bring to a boil. Reduce the heat and simmer for about 8 minutes, skimming the froth from the surface.

ADD THE SUGAR AND STIR TO DISSOLVE, then boil for 8 minutes. Pour the hot compote into a large sterilized preserving jar (or some small jars). As soon as it is cold it is ready to eat. Store in the refrigerator for up to 3 months.

I love cucumber salad. The sweet and sour flavor takes me back to my childhood vacations at the beach, staying with my grandparents. My grandmother would serve cucumber salad almost every day during spring and summer. She would reuse the dressing and just add freshly cut cucumber. This combination of dishes is also perfect served as a buffet at a party.

Veal with baked rhubarb, sweet and sour cucumber salad, and barley salad *(Serves 4)*

CUCUMBER SALAD
1¼ cups distilled vinegar
Generous ⅓ cup superfine sugar
1 cucumber, cut into paper-thin slices

VEAL
1 (1¾-pound) veal rump roast
Salt and pepper

BAKED RHUBARB
5 spring rhubarb stalks, trimmed and cut into ¼-inch pieces
2 tablespoons superfine sugar

BARLEY SALAD
Scant 1½ cups pearl barley
1 red onion, minced
¼ cup minced fresh flat-leaf parsley,
⅔ cup raisins, coarsely chopped

MAKE THE CUCUMBER SALAD. Combine the vinegar and sugar in a pan. Bring to a boil, reduce the heat, and simmer for 5 minutes, stirring the mixture to make sure all the sugar dissolves. Set aside to cool.

PLACE THE CUCUMBER SLICES IN A BOWL. Pour over the vinegar-sugar mixture, mix well, and refrigerate until ready to serve.

MEANWHILE, ROAST THE VEAL. Preheat the oven to 400°F. Score the fat on top of the veal rump roast into a diamond pattern and rub thoroughly with salt and pepper. Roast for 30 minutes, or until an instant-read thermometer registers 140°F (medium) or 175°F (well done).

MAKE THE BARLEY SALAD. In a pot, boil the barley in salted water for 20 minutes. Cover, remove from the heat, and let rest for 10 minutes.

DRAIN THE BARLEY THOROUGHLY, transfer to a large bowl and—while still hot—add the onion. Mix well and let cool. Add the parsley and raisins and season with salt and pepper.

PREPARE THE RHUBARB. Fold the rhubarb gently into the sugar so it is just about coated. Place in an ovenproof dish.

WHEN THE MEAT IS DONE, remove from the oven and let rest for 10 minutes. Meanwhile, decrease the oven temperature to 350°F and bake the rhubarb for 10 minutes, or until tender.

CARVE THE VEAL INTO SLICES and serve with the baked rhubarb, cucumber salad, and barley salad.

At the beginning of spring, rhubarb is pink and make a pink-colored cordial, but as the season progresses, the darker rhubarb produces a red cordial. It tastes wonderful diluted with still water, sparkling water, or Champagne. The dessert below is to die for, and you can serve it all year-round, just by switching the rhubarb for berries or other fruit. In summer, I prepare it with strawberries and raspberries, in fall with apples, and during winter with dried prunes and figs.

Rhubarb cordial *(Makes 6 cups)*

4 pounds rhubarb, trimmed and cut into 2-inch pieces
3½ cups water
3½ cups superfine sugar

RINSE THE RHUBARB IN COLD WATER and drain well. Combine the rhubarb and water in a saucepan and bring to a boil, then reduce the heat and simmer for 30 minutes.

LINE A STRAINER WITH CHEESECLOTH AND STRAIN THE COOKING LIQUID THROUGH IT. Transfer the liquid to a clean pot and bring to a boil with the sugar, stirring so that the sugar dissolves. Skim any froth from the surface and let simmer for 10 minutes.

POUR THE HOT LIQUID INTO STERILIZED BOTTLES and seal. When the cordial has cooled, store it in the refrigerator. To serve, mix one part rhubarb cordial with two parts cold water and serve over ice.

Rhubarb trifle *(Serves 6)*

MACAROONS
2 egg whites
½ cup superfine sugar
⅔ cup whole almonds

MAKE THE MACAROONS. Whisk the egg whites until they form stiff peaks. Add the sugar—just 2 tablespoons at a time—beating well after each addition. Process the almonds in a food processor until very finely ground, then fold into the meringue mixture.

RHUBARB
1 pound rhubarb, trimmed and cut into ¾-inch pieces
½ cup superfine sugar

PREHEAT THE OVEN to 350°F. Line a baking sheet with parchment paper and use a teaspoon to spoon about 25 small pyramids of the almond mixture onto it, keeping them a few inches apart. Bake for about 15 minutes, or until golden brown. Carefully lift the parchment paper from the sheet with the macaroons still on it and transfer to a wire rack to cool. (You can do this a few days in advance and store the macaroons in an airtight tin.) Reduce the oven temperature to 300°F to cook the rhubarb.

CREAM
1 vanilla bean
2 egg yolks
2 tablespoons superfine sugar
1¼ cups heavy cream

MAKE THE RHUBARB. Rinse the rhubarb in cold water and drain well. Place in an ovenproof dish and stir in the sugar. Bake for 15 minutes, or until tender. Remove from the oven and let cool.

MAKE THE CREAM. Cut the vanilla bean in half lengthwise and scrape out the seeds with the tip of a knife. Put the seeds in a bowl with the egg yolks and sugar and beat until pale and fluffy. In a separate bowl, whip the heavy cream until it forms soft peaks. Fold it into the egg mixture. Place in the refrigerator to chill.

FINISH THE TRIFLE. You can either do it immediately so that the layers become soft and melded, or wait until just before serving so that the trifle is fresh and crunchy. Break the macaroons into small chunks. Spoon a layer of cream into four serving glasses. Add the rhubarb, then the macaroons. Repeat the layers so that there are two of each ingredient. Finish with one more layer of cream.

June

In June, we celebrate midsummer night, the longest evening of the year. It does not get dark at all

on summer nights in the northernmost areas of Scandinavia, while in other parts it will stay light

until around midnight. Summer begins in June and is a busy month for cooks, with lots of

wonderful things to do. We usually get the first strawberries and new potatoes around midsummer.

However, elderflowers have to be gathered as soon as they blossom because the season is short.

Tiny bay shrimp live in bay areas around Denmark and are caught during the summer. In coastal areas in the northeast of the United States similar tiny shrimp may be available. If you cannot obtain them, use the smallest shrimp you can find. Bay shrimp have a very delicate taste and so should be eaten as freshly and simply as possible. I like them with caraway seed bread. Caraway is a common spice in Scandinavian kitchens and also used in aquavit and cheese. This traditional loaf tastes best the same day it is baked.

Bay shrimp with homemade mayonnaise (Serves 4)

1 pound cooked bay shrimp
Butter
Caraway Seed Bread (below)
Soft green lettuce leaves
4 slices lemon
Dill sprigs, for garnish

MAYONNAISE
2 egg yolks
2 tablespoons lemon juice or vinegar
1 teaspoon Dijon mustard
small clove garlic, crushed
Salt and pepper
1¼ cups extra-virgin olive oil

PEEL THE SHRIMP, or let your guests peel their own at the table. It takes time but it's fun and you can have a nicely chilled bottle of Alsace wine at the same time.

MAKE THE MAYONNAISE. In a small blender, combine the egg yolks, lemon juice (or vinegar), mustard, garlic, and salt and pepper and blend for 5 minutes. Slowly add the olive oil drop by drop, blending until the mixture starts to thicken. Do not add the oil too quickly. Continue until the mayonnaise is thick and smooth, then adjust the seasoning.

SPREAD THE BUTTER ON SLICES OF CARAWAY SEED BREAD. Cover with the lettuce, then the shrimp. Top with the mayonnaise and garnish with a slice of lemon and some dill.

Caraway seed bread (Makes 1 loaf)

Generous ⅓ cup lukewarm water
1 ounce fresh yeast
Generous 1 cup buttermilk
3½ cups all-purpose flour, plus extra for dusting
1 tablespoon caraway seeds
1 teaspoon salt
1 teaspoon superfine sugar

GLAZE
1 egg, beaten
1 tablespoon caraway seeds

PUT THE WATER IN A MIXING BOWL, add the yeast, and stir to dissolve. Add the buttermilk and stir again. In another bowl, sift together the flour, caraway seeds, salt, and sugar. Stir the dry ingredients into the yeast mixture, working the dough until it comes cleanly away from the edge of the bowl.

DUST A COUNTER WITH FLOUR and knead the dough for about 5 minutes. Return the dough to the bowl, cover with a dish towel, and set aside at room temperature to rise for 1 hour.

SHAPE THE RISEN DOUGH INTO A LOAF and place on a baking sheet lined with parchment paper. Let the bread rise again for 20 minutes. Preheat the oven to 400°F. Brush the bread with the beaten egg and sprinkle with caraway seeds. Bake for 40 minutes, or until the bread sounds hollow when you knock on its base.

LET THE BREAD COOL ON A WIRE RACK. It tastes best when freshly baked or, alternatively, if toasted the next day.

MIDSUMMER NIGHT. Midsummer night is celebrated in Sweden on June 22. It is a national holiday and the Swedes dance around the Maypole (majstang). In Denmark, midsummer night is more informal. On the evening of June 23, friends and family come together for a nice meal, preferably at the beach. Afterward, everyone goes to see the bonfires and the witch being sent off on her broom to Bloksbjerg. This is a perfect meal to share with friends on such a night. Pile the jumbo shrimp on serving dishes and pass them around. Let everybody tuck in, have a good time, and enjoy the informal atmosphere, good wine, and lovely company.

Jumbo shrimp with herb mayonnaise *(Serves 8)*

40 raw jumbo shrimp
2 lemons, sliced

HERB MAYONNAISE
4 egg yolks
2 tablespoons lemon juice
2 tablespoons chopped fresh chervil
2 tablespoons chopped fresh flat-leaf parsley
1 teaspoon Dijon mustard
1 clove garlic, crushed
Salt and pepper
2½ cups extra-virgin olive oil

MAKE THE HERB MAYONNAISE. Put the eggs yolks in a small blender. Add the lemon juice, chervil, parsley, mustard, garlic, and salt and pepper and blend for 5 minutes. Slowly add the olive oil, drop by drop, blending until the mixture starts to thicken. Do not add the oil too quickly. Continue until the mayonnaise is thick and smooth, then adjust the seasoning.

COOK THE SHRIMP UNDER A MEDIUM-HOT BROILER OR ON A BARBECUE for about 10 minutes, turning them two or three times, until they are firm when broken open. Serve immediately with the herb mayonnaise, garnished with the freshly sliced lemon.

IF YOU WANT TO SERVE THE SHRIMP AS A MAIN COURSE, double the quantity of shellfish and serve with the mayonnaise, a nice loaf of bread, and a fresh, crisp salad.

Lamb can be eaten all year-round, but for me it is a tradition to serve it on midsummer night with new potatoes and a summer cabbage salad with fresh peas—all the best ingredients of the season. You can ask your butcher to bone the leg of lamb for you.

Grilled leg of lamb with garlic and tarragon *(Serves 8)*

1 boned leg of lamb
Salt and pepper
10 tarragon sprigs
6 cloves garlic

HEAT A GRILL to medium.

LAY OUT THE LEG OF LAMB ON THE COUNTER. Sprinkle with salt and pepper, then cover with the tarragon and garlic. Fold up the meat and tie it at regular intervals with a piece of kitchen string to help it keep its shape.

LAY THE MEAT ON THE GRILL and cover with the lid. Cook for about 2 hours, or until an instant-read thermometer registers 160 to 175°F, taking care that the lamb does not burn underneath.

WHEN THE LAMB IS DONE, LET IT REST for 10 minutes before carving. Serve with the salads on page 102.

Elderflower has the taste of summer freshness. It is a bit like the feeling you get when the sun is shining on an early morning in the countryside and a gentle breeze is blowing. When beautiful elderflowers bloom, you know that summer is here and it is time to prepare elderflower cordial.

Elderflower cordial *(Makes 8 cups)*

40 elderflower clusters
3 lemons, sliced
2½ ounces citric acid
4 pounds superfine sugar
8 cups water

PUT THE ELDERFLOWERS, LEMONS, AND CITRIC ACID IN A VERY LARGE HEATPROOF BOWL. Combine the sugar and water in a pan and bring to a boil, stirring until the sugar has dissolved. Pour the syrup over the elderflowers, cover with a dish towel, and let rest for 3 to 5 days.

STRAIN THE MIXTURE, DISCARDING ALL THE SOLIDS. Pour any cordial that you are not going to use immediately into sterilized bottles and store them in a cool, dark place. To use the cordial, dilute to taste with still or sparkling water or Champagne and serve with slices of lemon.

SUMMER SALADS. Fresh, crunchy cabbage makes a delightful salad in early summer and the recipe below pairs it with some of the best ingredients of the season. New potatoes are a real treat in Scandinavia, too. They are tiny and have a fresh, light taste. Once cooked, which doesn't take long, they stay firm and the skin comes off very easily. They taste fantastic served with cold butter and salt on a piece of rye bread—very easy and very delicious.

Green cabbage with dill and peas *(Serves 8)*

2 green cabbages, cut into thin strips
⅔ cup almonds (optional)
1 bunch dill
1 pound fresh shelled peas

DRESSING
Juice of 1 lemon
1 tablespoon honey
⅓ cup vegetable oil
Salt and pepper

RINSE THE CABBAGE STRIPS THOROUGHLY then set aside to drain. If using the almonds, roast them in a 325°F oven for about 10 minutes or until the almonds are lightly browned. Let cool, then chop.

CHOP OFF THE TOP OF THE BUNCH OF DILL TO USE IN THE SALAD; reserve the rest for another recipe. Combine the cabbage, almonds, peas, and dill tops in a large salad bowl and toss.

MAKE THE DRESSING. Stir together the lemon juice and honey, then slowly add the oil. Season with salt and pepper. Toss the salad with the dressing just before serving.

Potato salad with fresh herbs and green onions *(Serves 8)*

4 pounds small new potatoes
¼ cup white wine vinegar
5 green onions, cut into ¼-inch pieces
1 small bunch fresh flat-leaf parsley, chopped
1 large bunch fresh chervil, chopped
4 bunches chives, minced
2 tablespoons minced fresh mint
¼ cup olive oil
Salt and pepper

SCRUB THE POTATOES AND BOIL IN A LARGE POT of salted water until soft but still firm. Drain and put in a large bowl.

ADD THE WHITE WINE VINEGAR AND GREEN ONIONS to the bowl, mix gently, and let cool.

JUST BEFORE SERVING, add the parsley, chervil, chives, olive oil, and salt and pepper.

Strawberries are divine. We have many varieties that grow very well in our climate. They are, in general, small with a very sweet flavor. Once picked, they do not last long and therefore have to be eaten right away. Their season is very short too. It starts around midsummer and lasts for about 3 or 4 weeks. It is best to serve them cold with sugar and cream.

Strawberries and cream *(Serves 8)*

6 pounds small, sweet strawberries, hulled
¼ cup superfine sugar
3 cups cold heavy cream

RINSE AND DRY THE STRAWBERRIES. Serve in a large bowl with sugar and cream on the side, letting your guests help themselves.

Meringues with strawberry-mint salsa *(Makes 10)*

MERINGUES
4 egg whites
1 cup superfine sugar
1 teaspoon vinegar
Vegetable oil, for brushing

STRAWBERRY-MINT SALSA
1 pound strawberries, hulled and cubed
10 fresh mint leaves, minced
⅓ cup Elderflower Cordial (page 100)
¾ cup heavy cream

MAKE THE MERINGUES. Put the egg whites in a large clean bowl and whisk with an electric mixer until they form stiff peaks. Add the sugar one spoonful at a time, whisking after each addition. (This takes time. For the perfect result, whisk for about 10 minutes or until the sugar completely dissolves and the meringue is glossy.) Finally, add the vinegar and whisk again.

LAY A PIECE OF PARCHMENT PAPER on a baking sheet and brush lightly with oil. Fit a pastry bag with a ¼-inch plain tip and fill with the meringue mixture. Pipe out ten round bird's nests, 2¾ inches in diameter, on the parchment paper, keeping them well spaced.

PREHEAT THE OVEN to 300°F. Bake the meringues for 5 minutes. Reduce the heat to 250°F and continue to bake for another 20 minutes, or until pale white and firm. Let the meringues cool on a wire rack.

MAKE THE SALSA. Put the strawberries and mint in a bowl and pour over the elderflower cordial. Mix together gently and set aside. Whip the cream until it forms soft peaks.

PLACE A MERINGUE ON EACH PLATE, add some whipped cream, and top with some of the strawberry-mint salsa. Serve immediately.

This soft, breadlike cake originated in Funen, Denmark. I think it deserves to become world famous. Sweet and tender and best the same day it is baked, it is traditionally eaten in the morning or with the afternoon coffee, but I also think it is perfect with a cup of tea. The only problem with this cake is that I can eat almost half of it all by myself.

Brunsviger *(Serves 10)*

Generous 1 cup lukewarm whole milk
2 ounces fresh yeast
2 eggs
6 tablespoons butter, melted
3½ cups all-purpose flour
2 tablespoons superfine sugar
Pinch of salt

GLAZE
¾ cup packed dark brown sugar
1 cup butter

POUR THE MILK INTO A BOWL, add the yeast, and stir with a wooden spoon until the yeast has dissolved. Add the eggs and mix well, then add the melted butter.

SIFT THE FLOUR WITH THE SUGAR AND SALT then stir the dry ingredients into the yeast mixture to make a dough. When the dough comes cleanly from the edge of the bowl, transfer to a floured counter and knead for about 5 minutes. Return the dough to the bowl and let rise at room temperature for 30 minutes.

LINE A 16 BY 20-INCH BAKING DISH WITH PARCHMENT PAPER and press the dough evenly in the dish. Cover with a dish towel and let rise again for 15 minutes.

MAKE THE GLAZE. Melt the brown sugar and butter together in a pan, stirring until the mixture is smooth and the sugar is no longer crunchy. Do not let it boil.

PREHEAT THE OVEN to 400°F. Press your fingers down into the risen dough, making small indentations across the surface. Spread the glaze evenly over the dough, leaving a ½-inch border. Bake for 25 to 30 minutes, or until the sugar has melted, and is brown and sticky. Let the brunsviger cool a little before cutting into pieces and serving.

July

The Scandinavian countryside can be many different things, from romantic and bountiful to austere and rugged. There are lakes, mountains, and mile after mile of forest. The habitat is diverse for such a small area of the world, and with Scandinavia's very long coastline, you are usually not far from the sea. At the height of summer, roses bloom and all the summer vegetables are readily available. In July we have raspberries, red currants, and cherries too.

BREAKFAST. Breakfast is an important meal in the northern part of the world. You cannot just eat a croissant and have a coffee on your way to work. We have a long tradition of heavy meals in the morning, although nowadays breakfast is becoming lighter. The perfect summer breakfast is yogurt with rysteribs—that is, "shaken" red currants—and bread crumbs: fresh, sweet, and very healthy because the fruit has a high level of vitamin C.

Yogurt with shaken red currants and rye bread topping *(Serves 8 to 10)*

SHAKEN RED CURRANTS
2¾ cups red currants, stems removed
1 cup supefine sugar

RYE BREAD SPRINKLES
4 ounces dry rye bread
2 tablespoons brown sugar

FOR SERVING
Low-fat yogurt

MAKE THE SHAKEN RED CURRANTS. Rinse the red currants in cold water and drain well. Spread them out on a large tray and sprinkle with the sugar. Shake the tray and then let stand until the sugar has dissolved (it takes a couple of hours), shaking the tray occasionally.

WHEN THE SUGAR HAS DISSOLVED, pour the mixture into a sterilized preserving jar, seal tightly, and store in the refrigerator for up to 3 weeks.

MAKE THE RYE BREAD SPRINKLES. Preheat the oven to 225°F. Break the rye bread into small pieces. Spread them out on a baking sheet and toast in the oven for 15 minutes. Let the crumbs cool before mixing with the brown sugar. Store in an airtight jar in a cool, dark cupboard.

TO MAKE YOUR EVERYDAY HEALTHY BREAKFAST, spoon a portion of low-fat yogurt into a bowl. Cover with 2 tablespoons of the shaken red currants and sprinkle with the rye bread sprinkles. Enjoy.

Red currant and strawberry smoothies *(Serves 4)*

3 cups yogurt
1¾ cups red currants, stems removed
2 cups strawberries, hulled
2 tablespoons honey
1 banana, cut into chunks
10 ice cubes

COMBINE ALL THE INGREDIENTS IN A BLENDER and puree for 3 to 5 minutes, until smooth. Serve immediately in glasses with a drinking straw in each.

Mackerel is perfect for everyday food in summer as it is inexpensive, healthy, and easy to prepare. When you pan-fry mackerel in butter, the skin becomes crisp and tastes delicious. Serve it with a fresh tomato salad and tiny baked potatoes. The dressing here has a sour taste that goes well with the fatty mackerel—if you prefer it sweeter, add some honey.

Fried mackerel with fresh summer salad *(Serves 4)*

POTATOES

1½ pounds small new potatoes

1 lemon, sliced

¼ cup olive oil

Salt and pepper

SALAD

4 ripe tomatoes, cut into wedges, then halved

1 cucumber, diced

1 small white onion, very thinly sliced

2 tablespoons white wine vinegar

1 teaspoon Dijon mustard

Pinch of sugar

¼ cup olive oil

MACKEREL

4 small fresh mackerel

2 tablespoons butter

Lemon wedges, for serving

MAKE THE POTATOES. Preheat the oven to 400°F. Put the potatoes in a baking dish with the sliced lemon. Drizzle with the olive oil, sprinkle with salt and pepper, and mix well. Bake for 45 minutes, or until golden brown.

MEANWHILE, MAKE THE SALAD. Put the tomatoes, cucumber, and onion in a bowl. Mix together the vinegar, mustard, sugar, and olive oil and fold the dressing into the salad.

MAKE THE MACKEREL. Season the fish with salt and pepper. Heat the butter in a large skillet and pan-fry the mackerel for about 5 minutes on each side. To check if cooked, lift the flap of the fish; the flesh should be white and tender. Serve the mackerel immediately with the tomato salad, baked potatoes, and fresh lemon to squeeze over the fish.

When meat is brined, it enhances the flavor and gives it a firmer, yet still tender, texture. In summer, I like to serve a lightly brined chicken with fresh tomatoes, which are red and full-flavored at this time of year. I grow four different kinds of mint in my small urban backyard and I therefore use a lot of it in salads, herb teas, and dressings.

Lightly brined chicken with tomato-mint salad and beet salad *(Serves 6 to 8)*

BRINE AND CHICKEN
6 cups water
6 tablespoons salt
6 tablespoons superfine sugar
15 fresh thyme sprigs
1 large chicken

MAKE THE BRINE. Put the water, salt, and sugar in a large pot and bring to a boil, whisking until the sugar and salt has dissolved. Turn off the heat and let the brine cool. Add the thyme.

TAKE TWO LARGE PLASTIC BAGS AND FIT ONE INSIDE THE OTHER. Put the chicken in the inner bag, then pour in the brine. Close the inner bag, trying to remove as much of the excess air as possible, then close the outer bag, knotting both securely. Lay the chicken in a baking dish and leave in the refrigerator overnight.

BEET SALAD
1 pound beets
2 tablespoons olive oil
Juice of 1 lime
3 tablespoons freshly grated horseradish
1 teaspoon superfine sugar
Salt and pepper

THE NEXT DAY, PREHEAT THE OVEN to 350°F. Take the chicken out of the bags, wipe it with a paper towel, and place in the baking dish. Roast for 1 hour 30 minutes, or until an instant-read thermometer registers 175°F.

MEANWHILE, MAKE THE BEET SALAD. Put the beets in a pan with enough water to cover. Boil for 20 minutes or until just tender. Place them in cold water and leave them until cool. Peel and cut into cubes. In a mixing bowl, whisk together the oil, lime juice, horseradish, sugar, and salt and pepper. Mix the cubed beets into the dressing and adjust the seasoning to taste.

TOMATO-MINT SALAD
10 fresh mint leaves
½ pound ripe cherry or Campari tomatoes, halved
1 cucumber, diced
1 tablespoon virgin olive oil

MAKE THE TOMATO-MINT SALAD. Mince half the mint leaves, leaving the other five whole. In a bowl, combine the tomatoes, cucumber, and both chopped and whole mint leaves. Mix in the olive oil and season with salt and pepper.

WHEN THE CHICKEN IS DONE, carve it into eight portions and serve with the salads.

Rygeost is a very special smoked, soft cheese produced in Denmark. It has the taste of summer sun and is ideal for a light lunch with cold beer.

Smørrebrød: smoked cheese salad on rye *(Serves 6)*

1½ pounds rygeost or smoked ricotta
1 cup homemade mayonnaise (page 92)
½ pound radishes, coarsely chopped
½ cucumber, seeded and cubed
¼ cup minced chives
Salt and pepper

FOR SERVING
Rye bread
Whole chives
Chopped radishes

MIX THE RYGEOST AND MAYONNAISE TOGETHER in a bowl, beating until there are no lumps remaining.

ADD THE RADISHES, CUCUMBER, AND CHIVES AND STIR TO MIX. Season with salt and pepper. Serve on rye bread, garnished with whole chives and chopped radishes.

In the good old days it was common to have a two-course dinner that was the main meal of the day. Meat was very expensive, so to make sure nobody went hungry you either had a fruit soup or a "porridge" such as this before the meal. During the summer, it was fruit porridge served with cold milk or cream. I love this recipe and in my family we enjoy it a great deal during summer both as a dessert and as an afternoon snack.

Fruit "porridge" with cold cream *(Serves 6)*

2 pounds red currants, stems removed
2 pounds strawberries, hulled
1 pound raspberries or black currants, stems removed
1¾ cups superfine sugar, plus extra for sprinkling
1 vanilla bean
¼ cup cornstarch
6 teaspoons ice-cold light cream or milk

RINSE THE RED CURRANTS AND STRAWBERRIES, but do not rinse the raspberries because they are too delicate. If you are using black currants, rinse them and nip off the little brown tops. Cut the strawberries into small pieces.

PUT ALL THE FRUIT IN A LARGE SAUCEPAN WITH THE SUGAR AND VANILLA BEAN. Bring to a boil and skim any froth from the surface, then decrease the heat and let simmer for 20 minutes.

DISSOLVE THE CORNSTARCH IN A LITTLE WATER. Raise the heat under the pot and add the cornstarch mixture to the porridge, stirring continuously as you bring it to a boil. As soon as the porridge reaches boiling point, turn off the heat.

POUR THE FRUIT PORRIDGE INTO A LARGE SERVING BOWL AND LET COOL COMPLETELY. Just before serving, sprinkle it with sugar. Serve with ice-cold cream or milk.

This is a fresh and simple dessert that can serve as a light meal or an afternoon snack on a summer day. Called kærnemælkskoldskål, this ice-cold soup is a favorite among children and anyone nostalgic for the food of their youth.

Cold buttermilk lemon soup with biscotti *(Serves 4)*

BISCOTTI

1¾ cups all-purpose flour

1 teaspoon baking powder

¼ cup superfine sugar

1 tablespoon grated lemon zest

9 tablespoons chilled butter, diced

½ beaten egg

¼ cup whole milk

BUTTERMILK SOUP

1 vanilla bean

3 egg yolks

6 tablespoons superfine sugar

2 tablespoons grated lemon zest

Juice of ½ lemon

6 cups buttermilk

1 whole lemon

MAKE THE BISCOTTI. Sift the flour and baking powder into a bowl and add the sugar and lemon zest. Rub the butter into the dry ingredients until the mixture resembles bread crumbs. Add the beaten egg and milk and stir to form a dough.

PREHEAT THE OVEN to 400°F. Knead the dough lightly on a floured counter, then roll it into a long, thin sausage. Cut the dough into small even-size pieces and use your hands to shape them into balls about the size of walnuts. Place on two baking sheets lined with parchment paper and bake for 7 minutes.

WHILE THE BISCOTTI ARE STILL HOT, CUT THEM IN TWO. Place them back on the baking sheets and bake again at 300°F for 20 minutes, or until golden brown. Let them cool on a wire rack then store in an airtight tin. They will keep for weeks.

MAKE THE SOUP. Split the vanilla bean lengthwise and scrape out the seeds with the tip of a knife. In a bowl, beat together the egg yolks, sugar, and vanilla seeds until pale and fluffy. Add the lemon zest and juice and the buttermilk. Chill for 1 hour.

CUT THE WHOLE LEMON INTO SLICES and add to the buttermilk soup just before serving. At the table, break the biscotti over the soup and eat immediately.

All Scandinavian cities have a bakery where you can buy freshly baked bread each day and a large range of cakes by the piece. In my family, however, we always have homemade layer cakes for birthdays. It is a good idea to bake the cake the day before you want to serve the layer cake.

Layer cake with strawberries *(Serves 12)*

SPONGE CAKE

Butter, for greasing
3 large eggs
¾ cup superfine sugar
Generous ¾ cup all-purpose flour
1½ teaspoons baking powder

CREAM FILLING

1 vanilla bean
1½ cups light cream
4 egg yolks
¼ cup superfine sugar
1½ tablespoons cornstarch
Generous ⅓ cup heavy cream

FRUIT FILLING

4 pounds strawberries, hulled and quartered
1 pound red currants, stems removed from half
Confectioners' sugar, for dusting

MAKE THE SPONGE CAKE. Preheat the oven to 350°F and grease a 10½-inch cake pan. Beat the eggs and sugar together with an electric mixer for at least for 10 minutes. Sift together the flour and baking powder, then fold gently into the egg mixture. Pour into the cake pan. Bake for 25 minutes, until the cake springs back when pressed gently in the middle. Let cool on a wire rack.

MAKE THE CREAM FILLING. Cut the vanilla bean in half lengthwise and scrape out the seeds with the tip of a knife. Combine the vanilla seeds and cream in a small pan and heat gently. Just before it starts boiling, turn off the heat. In a mixing bowl, whisk the egg yolks, sugar, and cornstarch together until pale and fluffy.

POUR ONE-THIRD OF THE HOT CREAM INTO THE EGG MIXTURE, whisking well. Pour the egg mixture into the pan and stir into the remaining cream. Whisk the mixture over low heat until it thickens, but do not let it boil. Once the mixture thickens, remove it from the heat and let cool. Whip the heavy cream until very stiff, then fold into the cooled vanilla cream.

FILL THE CAKE. Cut the sponge cake into three layers and place the bottom piece on a serving plate. Spread half the cream over it, then add half the strawberries and half the stemmed red currants. Add another layer of cake, the rest of the cream, and the rest of the strawberries and stemmed red currants. Cover with the last piece of cake, dust with confectioners' sugar, and decorate with the reserved red currants with their stems. Serve with tea and coffee.

August

There are a number of archipelagos in Norway and Sweden, such as the one around Stockholm. The islands are typically very rocky, with cliffs, valleys, lakes, and bays. The seascape is idyllic, calm, and very beautiful. In August the weather is always nice. That is, at least, the way I remember it. In the kitchen it is the time for mackerel, crayfish, dill, tomatoes, gooseberries, and even more red currants.

The crayfish season is short: about three weeks in August. Furthermore, Swedish crayfish are rare and expensive. People like to boil them in beer and eat them outside in the backyard with aquavit and beer. It is a wonderful way to celebrate life. I cook them in the morning and let them cool in the pot, then I pack a picnic basket and go down to the little lake near the house in Sweden where I often stay. It is so quiet and blissful that you almost forget everything around you and slip into a time-free zone.

Crayfish with bread and mayonnaise *(Serves 6)*

6 quarts water

6 cups dark beer such as stout or brown ale

5 dill sprigs, plus extra for garnish

4½ ounces salt

¼ cup superfine sugar

2 tablespoons peppercorns

2 tablespoons coriander seeds

1 lemon, sliced

6½ pounds live crayfish

FOR SERVING

Herb mayonnaise (page 94)

Rye bread

Crisp green salad

PUT ALL THE INGREDIENTS except for the crayfish in a large pot and bring to a boil. Once boiling, add the crayfish and return to a boil. Cook at a rolling boil for 1 minute, then turn the heat off and leave the fish in the pot until the liquid is cold.

TO SERVE, drain the crayfish and serve cold, garnished with dill and accompanied by homemade herb mayonnaise, rye bread, crisp green salad, beer, and aquavit.

This Scandinavian specialty can be made in hundreds of different ways. Fish cakes are suitable for dinner the day they are prepared, or served cold the next day with a salad or on rye bread. The remoulade is a must, and best when homemade. Many different types of fish can be used, but it is important that the fish be raw when forming the cakes.

Fish cakes with herb remoulade and dill potatoes *(Serves 4)*

HERB REMOULADE

1 tablespoon cornichons

1 teaspoon capers

1 cup homemade mayonnaise (page 92)

3 tablespoons crème fraîche

2 tablespoons chopped fresh chives

2 tablespoons chopped fresh tarragon

2 tablespoons minced carrot

1 tablespoon lemon juice

1 teaspoon Dijon mustard

1 teaspoon curry powder

Salt and pepper

FISH CAKES

1⅓ pounds white fish fillets

2 green onions, chopped

2 eggs

Generous ⅓ cup light cream

2 tablespoons minced fresh tarragon

3 tablespoons minced fresh parsley

Juice of ½ lemon

2 tablespoons potato flour

2 tablespoons butter

¼ cup vegetable oil, for cooking

Dill sprigs, for garnish

POTATOES

4 tablespoons butter

1¾ pounds cold boiled fingerling potatoes, peeled

¼ cup chopped fresh dill

MAKE THE REMOULADE. Chop the cornichons and capers together, then place in a mixing bowl with the remaining ingredients. Stir well and season with salt and pepper. Cover and put in the refrigerator until ready to serve.

MAKE THE FISH CAKES. Chop the fish fillets finely with a very sharp knife. Put in a mixing bowl with the green onions, eggs, cream, tarragon, parsley, and lemon juice and fold together gently. Add the potato flour, 2 teaspoons of salt, and 1 teaspoon of pepper and fold again.

HEAT THE BUTTER AND VEGETABLE OIL TOGETHER IN A LARGE SKILLET. Meanwhile, shape the fish mixture into 12 small balls using a spoon and your hands. Gently place the fish cakes in the skillet and cook over medium heat for about 4 minutes on each side, or until browned and cooked through.

MEANWHILE, MAKE THE POTATOES. In another skillet, melt the butter. When it starts to bubble, add the potatoes and pan-fry them slowly until golden. Fold in the chopped dill.

SERVE THE POTATOES WITH THE FISH CAKES AND HERB REMOULADE, garnishing the fish cakes with dill sprigs. A green salad would also be perfect here, or the sweet and sour cucumber salad on page 86.

Eggs are an important everyday food in many Scandinavian cultures. We have, for example, soft-cooked eggs for breakfast, and hard-cooked eggs on rye bread for lunch. We also eat a simple frittatas called æggekage, which is like a Spanish frittata without the potato. With bacon, chives, and fresh tomatoes on the side, this dish is served for lunch and dinner in summer, when the chives are cut from the backyard and the tomatoes are ripe and tasteful. It would be perfect for brunch.

Frittatas with tomatoes, bacon, and chives *(Serves 4)*

8 large eggs
Generous ⅓ cup whole milk
1 teaspoon all-purpose flour
Salt and pepper
2 tablespoons butter or
olive oil
12 pieces thickly sliced
bacon, 2–3 inches long,
preferably hand-cut
4 tomatoes, sliced
¼ cup minced fresh chives
4 slices rye bread

BREAK THE EGGS into a large bowl and beat thoroughly. Mix in the milk, flour, and salt and pepper and beat again until there are no lumps left.

DIVIDE THE BUTTER or oil between four small lidded skillets (or you could cook just one large frittata) and place over medium heat. Add the egg mixture and let it cook for 2 minutes, then turn the heat down to very low. Cover the skillets and cook for 8 minutes, or until cooked (see opposite). (If cooking the mixture as one large frittata, cook for 5 minutes uncovered, then 12 minutes covered.)

MEANWHILE, BROIL OR PAN-FRY THE BACON until golden and crisp. Place the sliced tomatoes and bacon on the frittatas, sprinkle with the chives, and serve with the rye bread. A cold beer is also very nice with this dish.

The classic dish, kalvespidsbryst, is normally served with gravy, but this lighter summer version, served with vegetables, still has lots of flavor. If there are any leftovers, slice the meat and serve it on rye bread with mustard and Pickled Cucumbers (page 148).

Veal brisket with sautéed vegetables *(Serves 4)*

3 pounds veal brisket
2 cups dry white wine
2 cups water
3 carrots
3 shallots
1 leek, sliced
3 cloves garlic
10 thyme sprigs
3 dill sprigs
1 tablespoon coarse sea salt
1 tablespoon peppercorns
5 bay leaves

POTATOES
2 pounds potatoes
¼ cup olive oil

VEGETABLES
¼ cup olive oil
2 cloves garlic, minced
½ pound mushrooms, quartered
1 pound broccoli florets, quartered or halved
4 tomatoes
Salt and pepper
2 ounces fresh horseradish, grated

PUT THE VEAL IN A LARGE PAN, pour over the wine and water, then add all the vegetables and flavorings. Bring to a boil and skim any froth from the surface. Reduce the heat to a simmer, half-cover the pan, and let it cook gently for 2½ hours, or until the meat falls apart when tested with a fork.

MAKE THE POTATOES. Preheat the oven to 400°F half an hour before the veal will be ready. Cook the potatoes in a large pan of salted water until tender, then drain. Slice the potatoes and put them in a baking dish. Stir in the olive oil and sprinkle with salt and pepper. Roast in the oven for 15 minutes, or until browned and cooked through.

MEANWHILE, MAKE THE VEGETABLES. Heat the olive oil in a large sauté pan and sauté the garlic and mushrooms together for 2 minutes. Add the broccoli florets and cook for 5 minutes. Take ⅓ cup broth from the meat and add to the sauté pan along with the tomatoes. Simmer for 3 minutes then season with salt and pepper.

CAREFULLY LIFT THE MEAT FROM THE BROTH AND PLACE ON A CUTTING BOARD. Carve it in slices and arrange on a serving dish. Cover the meat with the vegetables and sprinkle the horseradish over the top. Serve with the potatoes alongside.

Although this dish originated in Vienna, it has become a classic served throughout Europe and illustrates the extent to which European countries have influenced each other in developing food culture. It is important, I think, to broaden your horizons and at the same time preserve tradition. When it comes to food, I believe you have to be familiar with your own cuisine but also keep modifying it to a modern and healthy standard.

Wienerschnitzel with braised potatoes *(Serves 4)*

1½ pounds potatoes
4 thin veal scallops
4 cups fresh bread crumbs
Salt and pepper
2 eggs
8 tablespoons butter
4 lemon slices
8 anchovy fillets
2 tablespoons capers

BOIL THE POTATOES IN A LARGE SAUCEPAN of salted water until just tender, then drain. When they are cool enough to handle, peel and keep warm.

IF THE VEAL SCALLOPS ARE NOT ALREADY PAPER-THIN, pound each one with a meat mallet.

PUT THE BREAD CRUMBS IN A WIDE DISH OR PLATE and season with salt and pepper. Beat the eggs together in a bowl. Dip the scallops one at a time into the beaten eggs until completely coated, then lay them in the bread crumbs and press the crumbs into the veal, turning once, until evenly coated.

DIVIDE 4 TABLESPOONS OF THE BUTTER BETWEEN TWO SKILLETS and heat until melted. When hot, add the wienerschnitzel—two to each pan—and cook for about 3 minutes on each side, or until cooked through. Make sure that they stay golden and do not start to turn dark brown—if necessary, decrease the heat.

LIFT THE WIENERSCHNITZEL FROM THE SKILLETS and set aside in a warm place. Add the remaining butter to the skillets and let it melt, being careful not to burn it. Add the potatoes, stir gently to coat, then season with pepper.

ARRANGE THE WIENERSCHNITZEL ON FOUR PLATES. Place a slice of lemon, two anchovy fillets, and some capers on each one and serve immediately with the potatoes and butter sauce.

In August, there are so many soft fruits to choose from, and a perfect way to eat them is with vanilla custard. It is easier to prepare than ice cream, because you do not have to cook the cream, use an ice-cream maker, or go through the hassle of stirring every 15 minutes while the mixture is freezing. It can also be prepared days ahead of serving.

Vanilla custard with red currants *(Serves 4)*

1 vanilla bean
6 pasteurized egg yolks
⅔ cup superfine sugar
1¼ cups heavy cream
1 cup red currants

SLIT THE VANILLA BEAN LENGTHWISE and scrape out the seeds with the tip of a knife. Put the seeds in a bowl with the egg yolks and sugar and beat until pale and fluffy. Whip the heavy cream until it forms soft peaks, then very gently fold it into the egg mixture.

POUR THE MIXTURE INTO ONE OR MORE FREEZERPROOF CONTAINERS and freeze for 6 hours. The parfait is now ready. Serve with red currants or other fresh fruit on a summer day.

All summer I look forward to August because it is the season for gooseberries, which I buy in stores or collect from my mother's backyard. I boil them with sugar and vanilla to make a compote, then serve them with crêpes. When I make crêpes, I like to cook a big pile so that it seems that they will last forever.

Crêpes with gooseberry compote *(Serves 8)*

COMPOTE
1 vanilla bean
1 pound unripe gooseberries, trimmed
1 cup superfine sugar

CRÊPES
4 eggs
1¼ cups buttermilk
1 vanilla bean
1¾ cups all-purpose flour
2 teaspoons superfine sugar
1 teaspoon salt
1¼ cups whole milk
Butter, for cooking

MAKE THE COMPOTE. Halve the vanilla bean lengthwise and place in a pan with the gooseberries and sugar. Bring to a boil, then reduce the heat and simmer for 30 minutes. Pour the hot compote into sterilized preserving jars and seal tightly. When cool, store in the refrigerator.

MAKE THE CRÊPE BATTER. Beat the eggs together in a large mixing bowl. Add the buttermilk and beat again. Slit the vanilla bean in half lengthwise and scrape out the seeds with the tip of a knife. Sift the flour, sugar, and salt together, then add to the egg mixture and beat until smooth. Stir in the milk and vanilla seeds. Let the batter rest for 30 minutes before cooking the crêpes.

MELT A LITTLE BUTTER IN A SKILLET. When hot, add 5 tablespoons of batter to the skillet, twisting the handle gently to make a large, thin crêpe. Cook until golden on each side—it takes about 2 minutes. Set aside and repeat with the remaining batter. Stack the crêpes on a plate, interleaving them with waxed paper. They will stay warm like this for some time but, if you prefer, you can put them in a low oven. When the crêpes are all done, serve with the gooseberry compote.

September

Late summer or early fall is a beautiful time to visit Stockholm. The sunlight is still warm

and it does not get dark until 8 o'clock. You can still sit outside on some evenings. It is

time for tasty blueberries and earthy chanterelles, it is time to make preserves for winter,

and it is—because of the changing weather—time for braised dishes.

This is an easy way to make a very tasty pâté for lunch. Serve it with rye bread and preserved cucumber. It is also perfect as part of a buffet.

Chicken liver pâté with aquavit *(Serves 8)*

2 tablespoons butter
1 onion, chopped
3 cloves garlic, chopped
2 pounds chicken livers, trimmed and halved
10 thyme sprigs
¾ cup aquavit
1 cup chilled butter, cubed
1 cup reduced fat sour cream
2 tablespoons coarsely chopped mixed whole peppercorns
Salt and pepper

HEAT THE BUTTER IN A LARGE SKILLET, add the onion and garlic, and sauté until soft. Add the chicken livers and thyme and cook for 10 minutes, stirring occasionally until cooked through.

ADD THE AQUAVIT, raise the heat, and simmer for 2 minutes. Turn off the heat and leave the mixture in the pan for 5 minutes. Take out the thyme sprigs, then transfer the mixture to a food processor.

ADD THE CHILLED BUTTER, SOUR CREAM, AND PEPPERCORNS AND BLEND UNTIL SMOOTH. Season with salt and pepper. Transfer the mixture to a terrine or loaf pan and place in the refrigerator until the next day.

SERVE THE PÂTÉ with pickled cucumbers or beets (page 148), toasted bread, or rye bread.

Cucumbers are easily preserved and taste wonderful on smørrebrød. They can be enjoyed with cold meats and mustard, with various cooked meat dishes, or on burgers. Pickled beets can be eaten with smørrebrød, served as a condiment for Captain's Stew (page 52), or chopped and stirred into Biff Lindström (page 54).

Pickled cucumbers *(Makes 4 cups)*

4 cups distilled vinegar
2 cups superfine sugar
2½ teaspoons salt
Juice of 2 lemons
1 tablespoon peppercorns

3 to 4 cucumbers, cut into
¾-inch slices
1 large dill sprig, separated
into florets

IN A LARGE POT, BRING THE VINEGAR, SUGAR, SALT, AND PEPPERCORNS TO A BOIL, whisking until the sugar has dissolved. Turn the heat off, add the lemon juice and peppercorns, and let cool.

PACK THE CUCUMBERS AND DILL into a sterilized 1-quart jar, pressing them together.

POUR THE SPICED VINEGAR OVER THE CUCUMBERS AND SEAL TIGHTLY. The next day, there will be room in the jar to pack in more cucumbers. Do this, then let rest until the next day, when they will be ready to serve.

STORE THE PICKLES IN A DARK CUPBOARD UNTIL OPENING; thereafter keep them in the refrigerator and use within 2 months.

Pickled beets with star anise *(Makes 4 cups)*

2 pounds small beets
Salt

BRINE
3 cups distilled vinegar
½ cup superfine sugar
1 star anise
1 tablespoon peppercorns

PEEL THE BEETS AND BOIL THEM IN SALTED WATER for about 20 minutes—maybe a little less. Check them after 10 minutes: they have to have some bite and are best if not too soft.

WHILE THE BEETS ARE BOILING, make the brine. Bring the vinegar, sugar, star anise, and peppercorns to a boil in a pot, whisking until the sugar has dissolved. Turn the heat off and let cool.

DRAIN THE COOKED BEETS and, when cool enough to handle, cut into ¼-inch slices. Pack them in a sterilized jar, pressing them together. Pour over the brine and seal tightly. Let rest for 1 week before serving.

I love salmon, and this is the perfect way to eat it: cured in sugar and salt, then served with a mustard sauce (called fox sauce) and fresh dill, with an ice-cold beer alongside.

Gravlax with sweet mustard sauce *(Serves 8 to 10)*

1 (5½-pound) salmon fillet
2 tablespoons peppercorns
1 tablespoon coriander seeds
4½ ounces coarse salt
1 cup superfine sugar
2 bunches fresh dill, minced very finely, plus 6 sprigs extra

SAUCE
3 tablespoons brown sugar
3 tablespoons Dijon mustard
3 tablespoons white wine vinegar
2 tablespoons vegetable oil
1 bunch fresh dill, chopped

FREEZE THE SALMON FOR 24 HOURS before making the gravlax to ensure there are no harmful bacteria, then thaw.

REMOVE ANY PIN-BONES FROM THE SALMON and trim the edges of the fillet. Wipe off any scales with a paper towel and lay the salmon skin-side down on a sheet of plastic wrap.

CRUSH THE PEPPERCORNS AND CORIANDER SEEDS USING A MORTAR AND PESTLE and mix with the salt and sugar. Spread the minced dill evenly over the salmon, then cover with the spiced sugar mixture. Cut the salmon into 2 equal portions. Lay 3 of the dill sprigs over one piece then cover with the other piece of fish, laying it flesh-side down. Wrap in plastic wrap and let stand for 2 days in the refrigerator.

MAKE THE SAUCE. Place all the ingredients in a blender or food processor and process until the mixture is smooth.

TO SERVE, unwrap the salmon and wipe off all the salt and sugar mixture with a paper towel. The traditional cut starts diagonally at one corner of the salmon, and then works back toward the center of the fillet. Place the gravlax on a serving dish and garnish with the remaining dill sprigs. Serve with the honey mustard sauce and white or spelt bread.

In September, the weather can be everything from cold and rainy to like an Indian summer. On rainy days, when it gets a bit gloomy, I like to start some slow cooking—it gives me tremendous comfort when the aromas fill the kitchen and I'm reminded why I love living in a place with changing seasons.

Lamb shanks with apricots and spices and parsley mashed potatoes *(Serves 4)*

4 small lamb shanks
¼ cup olive oil
2 cups red wine
½ cup dried apricots
3 shallots, coarsely chopped
3 cloves garlic, coarsely chopped
1 cinnamon stick
10 whole cloves
2 rosemary sprigs
1 tablespoon grated lemon zest, plus extra for garnish
Salt and pepper
2 carrots, peeled
1 parsnip, peeled
1 turnip, peeled

MASHED POTATOES
3 pounds large potatoes
6 tablespoons minced fresh parsley
¼ cup olive oil
2 tablespoons butter
1 teaspoon grated mace

IN A LARGE DUTCH OVEN PAN OR CASSEROLE, brown the lamb shanks in the oil until golden brown all over. Add the red wine, apricots, shallots, garlic, cinnamon, cloves, rosemary, lemon zest, and enough water to partially cover the lamb. Bring to a boil and skim any froth that rises to the surface. Add salt and pepper, then reduce the heat to a gentle simmer, cover, and let cook for 2 hours, or until the meat is tender.

MAKE THE MASHED POTATOES. Peel and cube the potatoes and boil in salted water until tender. Drain, reserving some of the cooking liquid. Put the potatoes in a large bowl with the parsley, olive oil, butter, and mace and use a balloon whisk to mash the potatoes until the texture is only slightly lumpy. Add a little bit of the potato cooking water if the potatoes are not soft enough. Season with salt and pepper.

CUT THE CARROTS, PARSNIP, AND TURNIP INTO LARGE CHUNKS AND ADD TO THE LAMB. Let simmer for 15 minutes more, then season with salt and pepper. Put the lamb shanks on a serving dish with the vegetables and apricots, garnish with lemon zest, and serve with the mashed potatoes.

Horseradish has a very special sharp, peppery taste that is highly versatile. It can be used in sauces and dressings, or just shredded and sprinkled on a cold piece of meat served on a slice of bread with mustard. Horseradish grows very well in our climate. If you can't find chervil for the sauce, use parsley.

Chicken in horseradish and chervil sauce *(Serves 4)*

1 whole chicken
1 small whole onion
1 carrot
3 bay leaves
1 tablespoon peppercorns
1 tablespoon coarse salt

SAUCE
4 teaspoons butter
1 pound Jerusalem artichokes, peeled and sliced
1 fennel bulb, sliced
1 tablespoon all-purpose flour
6 tablespoons freshly grated horseradish
¾ cup heavy cream
¼ cup chopped fresh chervil
Salt and pepper

FOR SERVING
2 pounds boiled potatoes

PUT THE CHICKEN IN A LARGE CASSEROLE with the onion, carrot, bay leaves, peppercorns, and salt. Add enough water to cover the chicken, then bring to a boil and simmer for 1 hour, or until the meat is white. Carefully lift the chicken from the broth and let cool. Strain the broth and save 2½ cups for the sauce.

MAKE THE SAUCE. Melt the butter in a large pan. Add the sliced artichokes and fennel and cook for 2 minutes. Sprinkle the flour over the vegetables and stir until the flour and butter have combined. Pour in half the reserved chicken broth and stir until smooth. Add the remaining chicken broth and the horseradish and bring to a boil. Add the cream and salt and pepper and return the sauce to a boil, then decrease the heat to a simmer.

REMOVE THE SKIN AND BONES FROM THE CHICKEN. Break the meat into medium-size pieces. Stir the chicken and chervil into the sauce and let it simmer for a couple of minutes, or until the chicken is heated through. Season with salt and pepper and serve with boiled potatoes.

The chanterelle season starts in late August and, if it is a good year, goes on until October. The best mushrooms are collected in the woods. In Denmark we have professional pickers who, after they have been to the woods, will sell the chanterelles directly to stores and restaurants. Chanterelles are ruined if you wash them in water; brushing them clean is a lot of work, but worth it.

Chanterelle, bacon, and plum salad with blue cheese *(Serves 4)*

½ pound bacon, cubed
½ pound chanterelles
2 tablespoons olive oil
Salt and pepper
10 red or green plums, pitted and cut into wedges
6 cups mixed lettuce leaves
4½ ounces blue cheese, crumbled

DRESSING
¼ cup balsamic vinegar
½ teaspoon superfine sugar
2 tablespoons olive oil

COOK THE BACON UNTIL GOLDEN IN A SKILLET. Let drain on a piece of paper towel.

USE A DRY BRUSH TO CLEAN THE CHANTERELLES, then pan-fry them for 5 minutes in 1 tablespoon of the olive oil. Season with salt and pepper and let cool in the skillet.

SAUTÉ THE PLUMS FOR A MINUTE in the remaining 1 tablespoon oil.

MAKE THE DRESSING. Mix the balsamic vinegar and sugar together in a small bowl, then whisk in the olive oil until the mixture has emulsified (this will take a while as there is more vinegar than oil).

JUST BEFORE SERVING, combine the bacon, mushrooms, plums, and lettuce in a serving bowl. Pour the dressing over and toss gently. Add the blue cheese but do not toss the salad any more because it easily turns mushy.

SCANDINAVIAN CHEESE PLATTER. Knäkebröd is a very healthy flat bread and this version, made with rye flour, is easy to make at home. It is perfect with cheese and a great snack with honey. It will keep in an airtight container for up to a week.

Rye flat bread *(Makes 10)*

2 ounces fresh yeast
2 cups lukewarm water
1 teaspoon salt
2 teaspoons anise seed
1 tablespoon honey
Generous ⅓ cup sunflower oil
Scant 1½ cups rye flour
Scant 2½ cups rolled oats
1¾ cups all-purpose flour

DISSOLVE THE YEAST IN THE WARM WATER, then add the salt, anise seed, honey, and oil and mix well. Add the rye flour, oats, and half the all-purpose flour and mix for 5 minutes if using an electric mixer, or for 10 minutes if making the dough by hand. Sprinkle the rest of the all-purpose flour over the dough and let it rise for 15 minutes.

PREHEAT THE OVEN to 425°F and line a baking sheet with parchment paper. Knead the dough on a floured counter, then divide it into 10 equal pieces and roll each one into a very thin disc. In batches, lay the flat breads on the parchment paper and bake for 5 to 8 minutes, until crisp.

Walnuts in wine

½ cup superfine sugar
⅓ cup water
⅓ cup dessert wine, port, sherry, or red or white wine
1½ cups shelled walnuts

PUT THE SUGAR AND WATER IN A SAUCEPAN and bring to a boil, stirring to dissolve the sugar. Reduce the heat and simmer for 5 minutes. Add the wine and continue simmering for about 10 minutes, stirring occasionally, until the mixture develops a syrupy consistency.

MEANWHILE, IN A SEPARATE PAN, boil the walnuts in a generous amount of water for 1 minute, then drain. Mix the syrup and walnuts together and store in a sterilized jar until serving. Kept in the refrigerator, they can last for up to a month.

Scandinavian cheeses

ST. CLEMENS BLUE CHEESE FROM DENMARK
A lovely blue cheese produced on an island called Bornholm, it is made from cows' milk and has a mild, creamy taste.

JARLSBERG FROM NORWAY
This cows' milk cheese has a sweet, nutty taste. It is perfect in sandwiches, melted on burgers, used in salads, or simply served with flat bread and a glass of red wine.

VÄSTERBOTTEN FROM SWEDEN
A hard and dry cheese with a salty taste, it is suitable for pies, grating, or serving on flat breads with sweet walnuts.

We gather wild blueberries in the woods. The best way to eat them is fresh with a bowl of yogurt, or in a tart served warm with cold crème fraîche or sour cream.

Blueberry tart *(Serves 10)*

PIE DOUGH

2½ cups all-purpose flour
1 cup confectioners' sugar
½ cup chilled butter, cubed
1 whole egg plus 1 egg yolk
Butter, for greasing

FILLING

2 pounds blueberries
¾ cup superfine sugar

FOR SERVING

2 cups reduced fat
sour cream

MAKE THE PIE DOUGH. Sift the flour and confectioners' sugar together into a bowl. Rub the butter into the dry ingredients with your fingertips until the mixture resembles bread crumbs. Add the whole egg and yolk and stir until the dough comes together.

KNEAD THE DOUGH LIGHTLY ON A FLOURED COUNTER. Shape into a ball, wrap in plastic wrap, and let rest in the refrigerator for 1 hour.

LIGHTLY BUTTER a 10½-inch tart pan. Roll out the dough thinly on a lightly floured counter then use to line the tart pan. Trim the edges and let rest again in the refrigerator for 1 hour.

PREHEAT THE OVEN to 350°F. Cover the dough with a circle of parchment paper and weigh it down with dry beans or pie weights. Bake for 20 minutes. Take the tart shell out of the oven and remove the parchment paper and beans. Return the tart shell to the oven for another 10 minutes, or until light brown.

MAKE THE FILLING. Rinse the blueberries and mix them with the sugar. Remove the tart shell from the oven and increase the oven temperature to 400°F. Pour the blueberries into the tart shell and return to the oven for 20 minutes, or until the sugar has melted, and most of the blueberries are soft but some remain whole (see opposite).

REMOVE THE TART FROM THE OVEN and let cool for 10 minutes before serving with sour cream.

October

The season changes. The foliage of trees in woods and cities turns red, yellow, and brown, and fall leaves pile up under the trees. The sky is very beautiful with alternating clouds and sunshine. Days begin to shorten and the shades of daylight are shifting once again, this time to grayish colors. It is time for game, root vegetables, apples, hazelnuts, and walnuts—everything that gives comfort and pleasure. It is time to cook, and to tuck in.

In Scandinavia hot meals are frequently served with potatoes. They were consumed almost every day before rice and pasta were introduced. My grandparents had potatoes almost every day of their life. But during winter, I get tired of eating boiled potatoes and potato soup is, therefore, a nice alternative. Instead of bacon you can use crisp croutons of dark rye bread.

Potato soup with bacon and chives *(Serves 4)*

3 pounds potatoes, peeled and cut into large chunks
2 leeks, sliced
2 cloves garlic
2 bay leaves
1 tablespoon salt
1 tablespoon peppercorns
4 cups water
4 ounces bacon, diced
⅓ cup heavy cream
¼ cup chopped fresh chives
Grainy bread, for serving

PLACE THE POTATOES IN A LARGE SAUCEPAN with the leeks, garlic, bay leaves, salt, peppercorns, and water. Bring to a boil, then reduce the heat and simmer for 20 minutes.

WHILE THE SOUP IS COOKING, sauté the bacon until crisp and golden, then drain on paper towels to remove the excess fat.

REMOVE THE SOUP FROM THE HEAT AND LIFT OUT THE BAY LEAVES. Puree the mixture in a blender or food processor then return to the pan. Add the cream and heat through. Adjust the seasoning. Serve the soup very hot with the bacon and chives, plus grainy bread on the side.

This is an old recipe that has survived many generations, a wholesome and tasty meal that I prepare once every winter. The flavor is enhanced if the ragout is made the day before you serve it. If there are only four of you, you can serve it for dinner on two nights.

Oxtail ragout *(Serves 8)*

4 pounds oxtail pieces
1 cup butter
¼ cup olive oil
1 tablespoon all-purpose flour
2 cups red wine
4 shallots, coarsely chopped
6 cloves garlic, coarsely chopped
2 rosemary sprigs
4 bay leaves
1 tablespoon peppercorns
1 tablespoon coarse salt

FOR SERVING

5 parsnips, peeled and cut into long strips
¼ cup olive oil
½ pound chanterelles
2 tablespoons butter
Few flat-leaf parsley sprigs, for garnish

TRIM ANY EXCESS FAT from the oxtails and dry with paper towels. Melt the butter in a large, heavy casserole, then add the oil. Brown the oxtails, turning so they take on a nice golden color all over. Work in batches if you need to.

SPRINKLE THE FLOUR OVER the oxtails and turn until the flour is absorbed. Pour in the red wine, stir again, then add the shallots, garlic, rosemary, bay leaves, peppercorns, and salt. Add enough water to almost cover the oxtails and bring to a boil. Skim any froth that forms on the surface, then reduce the heat, cover, and simmer for 3 hours, or until the meat falls apart when tested with a fork. Remove the bay leaves.

ABOUT HALF AN HOUR BEFORE the oxtails will be ready, preheat the oven to 400°F. For the vegetable accompaniments, place the parsnips in a baking dish, add the olive oil, and turn until coated. Sprinkle with salt and pepper and roast for 20 minutes, or until firm to the bite.

CLEAN THE CHANTERELLES WITH A DRY BRUSH then pan-fry them in the butter for 5 minutes (make sure they're still crunchy). When the ragout is cooked, serve it with the chanterelles, roasted parsnips, and fresh parsley. You can also serve it with mashed potatoes.

Ham is traditional in Scandinavia, just as it is in Spain and Italy, but we are not as famous for it as they are. However, our hams are also of excellent quality and their salty taste goes well with this cheese tart. Skagen ham from Denmark is lightly smoked.

Swedish cheese tart with ham *(Serves 4)*

About 9 ounces puff pastry
Butter, for greasing
4 eggs
⅔ cup whole milk
10 ounces Västerbotten cheese, or strong hard cheese such as Cheddar, grated
½ teaspoon salt
Pepper

FOR SERVING
12 thin slices Skagen ham, Serrano ham, or prosciutto
Green salad

PREHEAT THE OVEN to 350°F. Roll out the pastry on a floured counter until thin. Use to line a buttered 8-inch tart pan (preferably one with a perforated bottom to help make the pastry crunchy).

IN A BOWL, BEAT THE EGGS AND MILK and stir in the cheese, salt, and lots of pepper. Pour the mixture into the tart shell.

BAKE FOR 45 MINUTES, OR UNTIL GOLDEN BROWN. Serve the tart warm with the ham and a crisp green salad.

In Scandinavia, this dish is made with reindeer. Reindeer fillet is very tender and low in fat; the taste is similar to moose. I like to add a bit of spice to it by covering it with lots of ground pepper and anise. Reindeer live in the northern part of Scandinavia. I do not recommend serving reindeer well done because it tends to be dry—medium-rare is best.

Venison with anise and pepper, potato-celery root gratin, and Brussels sprouts *(Serves 4)*

GRATIN

1⅓ *pounds potatoes, peeled and cut into large cubes*

1 *pound celery root, peeled and cut into cubes*

2 *cloves garlic*

3 *rosemary sprigs*

1 *tablespoon peppercorns*

1 *tablespoon salt*

4 *tablespoons butter*

4 *ounces Cheddar cheese, grated*

⅓ *cup heavy cream*

BRUSSELS SPROUTS

2 *tablespoons butter*

1 *pound Brussels sprouts, halved*

VENISON

1¾ *pounds venison fillet*

1 *tablespoon anise seed*

1 *tablespoon peppercorns*

Olive oil, for cooking

FOR SERVING

Cowberry Compote (page 84)

MAKE THE GRATIN. Place the potatoes and celery root in a large saucepan with the garlic, rosemary, peppercorns, and salt. Cover generously with water, bring to a boil, and cook for 30 minutes, or until the potatoes are tender. Drain, reserving some of the cooking liquid.

PREHEAT THE OVEN to 400°F. Discard the rosemary sprigs. Mash the potatoes and celery root with a balloon whisk. While the mixture is still lumpy, add the butter, cheese, and cream. Stir again—this time with a spoon—and season with salt and pepper. Divide between 4 small buttered soufflé dishes, or put it all in one large dish. Bake for 10 minutes or, if you are making this in advance and you don't want it to go cold, bake for 30 minutes.

MEANWHILE, COOK THE SPROUTS. Heat the butter in a skillet and pan-fry the sprouts for 5 minutes. Sprinkle with salt and pepper and keep warm.

COOK THE VENISON. Cut the fillet into 8 equal slices. Use a mortar and pestle to crush the anise seed and peppercorns and place them in a dish. Turn the venison in it to coat evenly. Heat the olive oil in a skillet and cook the venison slices for 3 to 4 minutes on each side, until medium-rare.

SERVE THE VENISON with the gratin, Brussels sprouts, and cowberry compote.

FALL SALADS. There are many ways to combine all the wonderful fruits and vegetables of fall—the only limit is your imagination. Hamburg parsley is a very popular root vegetable in Denmark that looks rather like parsnips; if you can't find any, substitute celery root.

Baked root vegetable salad *(Serves 4)*

2 beets
2 carrots
½ celery root
2 parsnips
2 Hamburg parsleys
¼ cup olive oil
Salt and pepper
¼ cup balsamic vinegar

PREHEAT THE OVEN to 350°F. Peel all the vegetables and cut lengthwise into strips. Place in a roasting pan, pour the olive oil over, and sprinkle with salt and pepper. Use your hands to mix the vegetables in the oil. Roast for 30 minutes, or until firm to the bite.

WHEN THE VEGETABLES ARE DONE, transfer to a serving bowl and stir in the balsamic vinegar. Adjust the seasoning with salt and pepper, then serve warm or cold.

Spelt salad *(Serves 4)*

½ pound whole spelt grains
½ celery root, diced
¼ cup olive oil
¼ cup minced fresh flat-leaf parsley
6 tablespoons chopped fresh curly parsley
¼ cup minced fresh chives
2 tablespoons white wine vinegar
Salt and pepper

SOAK THE SPELT GRAINS IN A BOWL OF COLD WATER for 1 hour, then drain. Place in a saucepan and cover with fresh water. Bring to a boil and cook for 30 minutes, or until soft but with a firm bite. Drain and let cool.

MEANWHILE, PREHEAT THE OVEN to 350°F. Roast the celery root in the olive oil for about 20 minutes until tender. While the celery root is still hot, mix it into the cooked spelt and let cool.

ADD THE CHOPPED HERBS AND WHITE WINE VINEGAR and season with salt and pepper before serving.

Jerusalem artichoke salad *(Serves 4 to 6)*

3 lemon slices
1⅓ pounds Jerusalem artichokes
1 teaspoon Dijon mustard
1 teaspoon superfine sugar
2 tablespoons cider vinegar
¼ cup walnut oil
½ pound grapes, seeded
1 cup walnuts, coarsely chopped
Salt and pepper

HAVE READY A BOWL OF WATER WITH THE LEMON SLICES. Peel the Jerusalem artichokes and cut them into very thin slices, adding them to the water as you go to prevent browning.

WHISK TOGETHER THE MUSTARD, SUGAR, VINEGAR, AND WALNUT OIL to make a dressing.

DRAIN THE ARTICHOKES WELL and place in a bowl with the grapes and walnuts. Fold in the dressing, season with salt and pepper, and serve immediately.

This is (still) the best apple dessert I have ever had and it is served cold. Apple is the dominating flavor but the dessert has a crunchy edge from caramelized croutons.

Apple trifle *(Serves 8)*

*3 pounds cooking apples,
peeled, cored, and cubed
1 vanilla bean
1 cup superfine sugar
½ pound stale bread, diced
4 tablespoons butter
¾ cup heavy cream*

PLACE THE APPLE CUBES IN A SAUCEPAN. Cut the vanilla bean lengthwise, then scrape the seeds out with the tip of a knife and add to the apples with ½ cup of the superfine sugar. Bring to a boil, then reduce the heat and simmer for 10 minutes. Stir the mixture to a lumpy apple sauce, then let cool.

TOAST THE BREAD PIECES IN A DRY SKILLET, stirring frequently, until they begin to take on some color. Add the butter and remaining ½ cup sugar and continue cooking and stirring so that the tiny croutons caramelize slowly and evenly, without burning.

IN A SERVING BOWL, preferably a glass one, alternative layers of apple sauce and croutons. Whip the cream until it forms soft peaks and use it to decorate the top of the dessert. Serve immediately or let it rest in the refrigerator for a couple of hours before serving.

You can buy soft, sweet cinnamon rolls all over Scandinavia in different variations, but the homebaked ones are the best, of course. They are perfect for a late breakfast or afternoon tea, or served with the hot apple drink below. I think hot drinks such as this are very romantic—the essence of everything that fall has to offer.

Cinnamon rolls *(Makes approximately 20)*

2 ounces fresh yeast
2 cups lukewarm milk
Scant ¾ cup softened butter
1 egg, beaten
6 cups all-purpose flour
2 teaspoons ground cardamom
½ teaspoon salt
¾ cup superfine sugar

FILLING
¾ cup softened butter
½ cup superfine sugar
4 teaspoons ground cinnamon

GLAZE
1 egg, beaten
Superfine sugar, for sprinkling

IN A LARGE BOWL, DISSOLVE THE YEAST IN THE WARM MILK USING A WOODEN SPOON. Mix in the butter, then add the egg and stir again. Sift together the flour, cardamom, and salt and add to the milk mixture with the sugar, stirring to form a dough. Keep stirring until the dough comes cleanly from the edge of the bowl.

KNEAD THE DOUGH ON A FLOURED COUNTER for about 5 minutes. Return it to the bowl, cover with a dish towel, and let rise for 30 minutes at room temperature.

MAKE THE FILLING. Mix the butter, sugar, and cinnamon together.

DIVIDE THE DOUGH IN HALF and roll each piece to a 16 by 12-inch rectangle. Spread the cinnamon filling over the tops. Starting with a long side, roll up each piece of dough into a wide cylinder and cut into 1-inch slices.

LINE BAKING SHEETS WITH PARCHMENT PAPER. Lay the cinnamon rolls on the paper, pressing down on each one so that they spread slightly. Cover and let rise for 20 minutes.

PREHEAT THE OVEN to 425°F. Brush the cinnamon rolls with the beaten egg and sprinkle with sugar. Bake for 12 to 15 minutes, or until golden brown. Let cool on a wire rack. Serve warm or cold with a nice cup of tea.

Hot apple drink with Calvados *(Serves 4)*

2 pounds crisp apples
½ cup superfine sugar
4 cups water
1 long cinnamon stick plus
4 short cinnamon sticks
⅓ cup Calvados
4 mint sprigs

CUT THE APPLES INTO FOUR WEDGES and place in a large saucepan with the sugar, water, and long cinnamon stick. Bring to a boil, then reduce the heat and simmer for 30 minutes.

STRAIN THE APPLE-FLAVORED LIQUID THROUGH A PIECE OF CHEESECLOTH. Pour it back into the cleaned pan and bring to a boil. Add the Calvados and turn off the heat.

POUR INTO 4 HEATPROOF GLASSES and serve with short cinnamon sticks and mint sprigs.

November

Winter has started in the north. Some areas are already covered in snow. In the south it is dark and there is no snow to light up the landscape. The days are shorter and you spend most of your time indoors with candles lit and fire in the fireplace. It is time for soup, pheasant, Sunday roast, and luxurious cakes.

Soup is perfect for everyday meals or as an appetizer. This one has a creamy taste—grilled scallops soaked in lemon complement it nicely.

Cauliflower soup with grilled scallops *(Serves 4)*

SOUP

2 tablespoons olive oil
1 onion, chopped
2 cloves garlic, chopped
2 tablespoons curry powder
1 large cauliflower, chopped
4 cups water
⅓ cup heavy cream
Salt and pepper

SCALLOPS

12 sea scallops
2 tablespoons olive oil
Juice of ½ lemon
8 watercress sprigs

MAKE THE SOUP. Heat the oil in a large saucepan. Add the onion, garlic, and curry powder and sauté lightly. Add the cauliflower and water and bring to a boil. Reduce the heat and simmer for 30 minutes, or until the cauliflower is tender.

BLEND THE SOUP UNTIL SMOOTH in a blender or food processor. Add the cream and season with salt and pepper.

MAKE THE SCALLOPS. Brush them with olive oil and sprinkle with salt and pepper. Heat a stovetop ridged grill pan. Cook the scallops for 3 minutes on each side. Take the scallops off the heat and pour some lemon juice over them.

ARRANGE THE SCALLOPS ON 4 SKEWERS and serve on the top of the soup, garnished with watercress.

Scandinavia is experiencing a beer revolution and the many different varieties of beer now available is very exciting. Many of these beers are good to use in cooking. The following recipe uses brown ale to marinate pork cheeks.

Pork cheeks in brown ale *(Serves 8)*

4 pounds pork cheeks
3 cups brown ale or similar dark beer
1 tablespoon coriander seeds
1 tablespoon peppercorns
3 tablespoons olive oil
10 thyme sprigs
Salt and pepper
1⅓ pounds potatoes, peeled and thickly sliced
3 carrots, peeled and thickly sliced
3 turnips, peeled and thickly sliced

IN A GLASS OR CERAMIC BOWL, marinate the meat in the brown ale, coriander seeds, and peppercorns for 12 hours or overnight.

THE NEXT DAY, REMOVE THE PORK FROM THE MARINADE. Heat the olive oil in a casserole and brown the meat on all sides. Add the liquid from the marinade, then the thyme and some salt. Reduce the heat and simmer for 1 hour.

ADD THE POTATOES TO THE CASSEROLE and simmer for 15 minutes. Add the carrots and turnips and continue cooking for another 15 minutes, or until the vegetables are tender. Season with salt and pepper, then serve just as it is—the taste is very full and aromatic.

Pheasant can be tender and delicious, especially if you cook it with perfection and love. On Saturday nights in the fall I like to cook pheasant, barded with good quality organic bacon and stuffed with bread and herbs, for close friends and family. When dinner is ready and the guests have arrived, I fetch some of my best red wine from the cellar and enjoy the pleasures of living in a part of the world where there are four very different seasons.

Braised stuffed pheasant with savoy cabbage, gravy, and potatoes *(Serves 4)*

STUFFING

2 slices bread, chopped
¼ cup chopped fresh
flat-leaf parsley
20 juniper berries, crushed

PHEASANTS

2 pheasants
12 slices bacon
1¼ cups red wine
¼ cup port wine
2 shallots, sliced
1 carrot, sliced
10 thyme sprigs
1 tablespoon peppercorns
1¼ cups water
¾ cup heavy cream

VEGETABLES

1¾ pounds fingerling potatoes
Salt and pepper
1½ to 2 tablespoons butter
1⅓ cups hazelnuts, chopped
1 small savoy cabbage, shredded
¼ cup water

MAKE THE STUFFING. Mix the bread and parsley with the juniper berries.

MAKE THE PHEASANTS. Preheat the oven to 400°F. Use the stuffing to stuff the cavities of the pheasants. Wrap the bacon slices around the birds and place them in a roasting pan. Pour over the red wine. Roast for 15 minutes. Reduce the heat to 350°F and add the port wine, shallots, carrot, thyme, peppercorns, and water. Tightly cover the pan with foil and roast for 35 minutes longer.

REMOVE THE PHEASANTS FROM THE OVEN, discard the foil, and stir in the cream. Return the pheasants to the oven and roast for 20 minutes longer. To check if done, insert a skewer into the leg; the juices should run clear.

MEANWHILE, MAKE THE VEGETABLES. Boil the potatoes in a large pot of salted water until tender, then drain. Once they are cool enough to handle, peel them. Keep warm until serving.

MELT THE BUTTER IN A SKILLET and sauté the chopped hazelnuts for a couple of minutes. Add the cabbage and water and sauté for a few minutes more, or until soft and tender.

CARVE THE PHEASANTS and season the sauce with salt and pepper. Serve the pheasants with the chunky vegetable sauce, cabbage, and potatoes.

Moose is eaten during the hunting season. The meat is dark red and can be used for various dishes such as hamburgers, stews, and tournedos. Traditional cowberry compote is a perfect match. If you can't buy moose, venison is a good substitute.

Moose tournedos with kale salad and cowberry compote *(Serves 4)*

SALAD

7 ounces kale, shredded

2 carrots, peeled and cut into thin sticks

2 apples, peeled, cored, and cubed

⅔ cup blanched almonds

1 tablespoon honey

4 tablespoons balsamic vinegar

2 tablespoons walnut oil

Salt and pepper

TOURNEDOS

2 tablespoons butter

4 tablespoons olive oil

4 moose tournedos

4 ounces chanterelles or other mushrooms

Cowberry Compote (page 84), for serving

MAKE THE SALAD. Mix the kale, carrots, and apples in a bowl.

TOAST THE ALMONDS IN A HOT DRY SKILLET, stirring constantly so that they do not burn. When lightly browned and fragrant, add the honey and let it caramelize. Add 2 tablespoons of the balsamic vinegar and simmer until the liquid has evaporated. Set the almonds aside to cool on a piece of parchment paper, then chop. Add the almonds to the kale salad with the walnut oil and remaining 2 tablespoons balsamic vinegar. Season the salad with salt and pepper.

MAKE THE TOURNEDOS. In a skillet, heat the butter and 2 tablespoons of the olive oil and pan-fry the tournedos for 5 to 6 minutes on each side, or until firm to the touch. Meanwhile, clean the chanterelles with a dry brush. Remove the tournedos from the skillet and set aside to rest. Add the remaining 2 tablespoons olive oil to the skillet and cook the mushrooms for 5 minutes.

SERVE WITH MOOSE TOURNEDOS WITH THE CHANTERELLES ON TOP and the salad and cowberry compote on the side.

This is one of very few dishes that my son and daughter, who normally disagree strongly on food, both claim as a favorite. It is filling and makes a nourishing family dinner when darkness is approaching, the rain is pouring down, and the temperature is getting colder and colder. This recipe will serve a family of four for two evenings.

Meatballs in curry sauce *(Serves 8)*

MEATBALLS

1 pound ground pork
1 pound ground veal
1 small onion, chopped
2 cloves garlic, crushed
Generous ¾ cup milk
⅓ cup all-purpose flour
1 tablespoon curry powder
5 teaspoons salt
Pepper
4 eggs
2 bay leaves

SAUCE

2 tablespoons butter
2 onions, chopped
2 cloves garlic, chopped
2 tablespoons curry powder
2 tablespoons all-purpose flour
¾ cup heavy cream
1 leek, sliced
2 carrots, peeled and cut
into large chunks
2 apples, cored and sliced

MAKE THE MEATBALLS. Combine the ground meats, onion, and garlic in a bowl. Add the milk, flour, curry powder, 2 teaspoons of the salt, and some pepper and mix together. Add the eggs and mix again for about 5 minutes so that the mixture is as light and fluffy as possible.

HEAT 4 TO 5 QUARTS WATER IN A POT. Add the bay leaves and remaining 3 teaspoons salt and bring to a boil. Meanwhile, use your hands to shape half the meat mixture into little balls about ¾ inch wide. Drop them in the water and simmer for 20 minutes, or until cooked through.

REMOVE THE MEATBALLS FROM THE BROTH WITH A SLOTTED SPOON AND PLACE ON A TRAY. Shape and cook the remaining meat mixture in the same way. Set all the meatballs aside until the sauce is done, reserving 3⅓ cups of the cooking liquid.

MAKE THE SAUCE. In another pot, melt the butter, add the onions, garlic, and curry powder, and cook for a couple of minutes. Add the flour and stir well. Add ⅓ cup of the meatball cooking liquid and stir until smooth. Pour in the rest of the cooking liquid and bring to a simmer.

ADD THE CREAM AND RETURN TO A BOIL. Reduce the heat, add the meatballs, leek, and carrots, and simmer for 5 minutes. Add the apples and continue cooking for 3 minutes. Season with salt and pepper and serve with rice.

Sunday lunch is popular all over the Western world. It is an old tradition that families meet after church to eat their best meal of the week. Meat is, therefore, an essential part of the tradition because in the past we did not eat meat every day. One cannot claim that church plays a big part in people's lives nowadays, and many traditions have changed in tandem with changes in the way we live our lives, but Sunday lunch is nice and I think we should fight to maintain this tradition.

Old-fashioned roast with potatoes and salsify (Serves 8)

1 boneless beef rib roast, about 9 pounds
2 tablespoons coarse sea salt
Pepper
5 shallots, peeled and halved
3 carrots, peeled and chopped
5 cloves garlic
3 rosemary sprigs
2 cups red wine
2 cups water

SAUCE
4 teaspoons butter
2 cloves garlic, chopped
10 ounces mushrooms, cut into wedges
1 tablespoon all-purpose flour
⅔ cup heavy cream

VEGETABLES
4 pounds potatoes
2 pounds salsify
Milk, for soaking
¼ cup olive oil

PREHEAT THE OVEN to 425°F. Trim any excess fat from the bottom of the roast. Score a diamond pattern in the top layer of fat and sprinkle with the coarse salt and some pepper. Place the roast in a large roasting pan. Arrange the shallots, carrots, garlic, and rosemary around the meat. Roast for 15 minutes.

REDUCE THE OVEN TEMPERATURE to 350°F and add the red wine and water to the pan. Continue roasting for 1 hour and 45 minutes, or until an instant-read thermometer registers 175°F. Add a bit more water now and then so the meat does not dry out.

WHEN DONE, TAKE THE ROAST FROM THE PAN AND SET ASIDE TO REST. Strain the pan juices into a glass bowl and let stand until the broth and fat separate. Discard the fat. Measure the broth and, if there is not 2½ cups, add some water.

MAKE THE SAUCE. Melt the butter in a skillet, add the garlic and mushrooms, and cook for 2 minutes. Add the flour and stir well. Add the broth from the roast and bring to a boil, then reduce the heat and simmer for 10 minutes. Add the cream and simmer for another 5 minutes. Season with salt and pepper.

MEANWHILE, MAKE THE VEGETABLES. Boil the potatoes in a large pan of salted water, then peel and keep warm. Peel the salsify and soak in milk to prevent discoloration.

HEAT THE OLIVE OIL IN A SKILLET and pan-fry the salsify for 5 minutes, then season with salt and pepper. Carve the meat and serve with the sauce, potatoes, and salsify.

Medaljer ("medals") are very popular cakes served for afternoon coffee. They are crisp and creamy, sweet, and fresh.

Medaljer *(Makes 10)*

CAKES
1½ cups all-purpose flour
½ cup confectioners' sugar
1 teaspoon lemon zest
1 cup chilled butter, chopped
½ beaten egg

FILLING
½ vanilla bean
2 crisp apples, peeled, cored, and cubed
½ cup packed natural brown sugar or Demerara sugar
¾ cup heavy cream

TOPPING
7 ounces good-quality semisweet chocolate
3 tablespoons butter

MAKE THE CAKES. Sift the flour and confectioners' sugar into a mixing bowl and add the lemon zest. Rub the butter into the dry ingredients until the mixture resembles bread crumbs. Add the egg and stir until the dough comes together in a ball. Wrap in plastic wrap and chill for 30 minutes.

PREHEAT THE OVEN to 425°F and line a baking sheet with parchment paper. Roll out the dough on a floured counter to a thickness of ⅟₁₆ to ⅛ inch. Use a 2½- to 2¾-inch pastry cutter or the rim of a glass to cut the dough into discs. Arrange on the parchment paper. Bake for 6 to 7 minutes, or until golden brown. Transfer carefully to a wire rack to cool.

MAKE THE FILLING. Cut the half vanilla bean lengthwise and scrape the seeds out with the tip of a knife. Put the apples in a pan with the brown sugar and vanilla seeds and bring to a boil, then reduce the heat and simmer for 20 minutes. Stir the apple mixture together to give a thick sauce, then cool.

MAKE THE TOPPING. Melt the chocolate and butter together in a double boiler and stir until smooth. Spread half the cake discs (medals) with the chocolate mixture, leaving a ⅟₁₆-inch border. Put aside to let the chocolate set. These are the upper medals.

WHIP THE CREAM UNTIL IT FORMS STIFF PEAKS. Take the remaining medals and place 1 teaspoon of apple sauce on each. Fit a pastry bag with a star-shaped tip and fill with the whipped cream. Pipe a ring of cream around the apple sauce. These are the lower medals.

PUT THE UPPER MEDALS ON TOP OF THE LOWER MEDALS so that they cover the apple sauce and whipped cream. Serve immediately with coffee or tea.

December

In Scandinavia we celebrate Christmas on the evening of December 24. If you go to church, you do so in the afternoon. After a very rich meal you are so full you cannot move, so of course you have to dance around the Christmas tree, which must be lit with real candles. Some families are more dedicated to carols than others. Finally, we open presents and have coffee, Danish butter cookies, homemade chocolates, oranges, and apples. It is a long but delightful evening if you happen to love Christmas, as I do.

SUNDAYS IN ADVENT. The four Sundays before Christmas are called "Sundays in advent." Many people will throw an afternoon party on one of these Sundays, getting together to bake cookies, make gingerbread houses, go skating, take a walk in the woods, play games, eat Christmas doughnuts (æbleskiver), and drink mulled wine. The butter-fried doughnuts are cooked in a special pan (called an aebleskiver pan and available from Williams-Sonoma) that has about ten ball-like indentations, but you could simply cook them like pancakes in a large skillet. Glögg is warm red wine with aquavit and spices. It is a lovely drink to serve when it is cold outside. Be careful with the aquavit, or leave it out altogether, to make the mulled wine a bit lighter, with a sweeter taste.

Christmas doughnuts *(Serves 10 to 12)*

1½ ounces fresh yeast
3⅓ cups lukewarm milk
4 cups all-purpose flour
2 teaspoons salt
1½ teaspoons ground cardamom
2 vanilla beans
2 tablespoons superfine sugar
4 eggs, separated
8 to 9 tablespoons butter

FOR SERVING
Confectioners' sugar
Raspberry jelly

DISSOLVE THE YEAST IN THE MILK IN A BOWL. In another mixing bowl, sift together the flour, salt, and cardamom. Slit the vanilla beans lengthwise, scrape out the seeds with the tip of a knife, and add them to the dry ingredients with the sugar.

WHISK THE EGG YOLKS INTO THE MILK MIXTURE—using an electric mixer if possible. Add the dry ingredients and beat to make a dough. In a separate bowl, whisk the egg whites until stiff, then fold them into the batter. Let stand for 40 minutes.

HEAT AN AEBLESKIVER PAN OVER MEDIUM HEAT. Put a little butter in each indentation and when it has melted pour in some of the batter. Cook for 3 to 5 minutes, or until golden underneath, then turn the doughnuts over so that they form a ball. Continue cooking for about 5 minutes, or until golden brown. Remove from the pan and repeat with the remaining butter and batter.

DUST WITH CONFECTIONERS' SUGAR and serve immediately with raspberry jelly and mulled wine.

Glögg *(Serves 8)*

2 cups water
1 cinnamon stick, smashed
1 tablespoon whole cloves
1 tablespoon dried orange zest
1 tablespoon coarsely chopped cardamom pods
2 bottles (750-miilliliter) red wine
4 tablespoons superfine sugar
2½ cups aquavit or vodka (optional)
1¼ cups raisins
1⅓ cups blanched almonds, chopped

PUT THE WATER IN A SAUCEPAN with the cinnamon stick, cloves, dried orange zest, and cardamom pods and bring slowly to a boil. Reduce the heat and simmer for 15 minutes. Turn the heat off and let stand for another 15 minutes. Strain through a strainer. Discard the spices and save the liquid.

IN A SAUCEPAN, combine the spiced liquid, red wine, and sugar and bring slowly to a boil. Reduce the heat and simmer for 10 minutes.

ADD THE AQUAVIT OR VODKA (IF USING), raisins, and almonds and simmer gently for 5 minutes, but do not let it boil. If you prefer a sweeter drink, add more sugar. Serve in tall glasses with spoons so that you can catch the raisins and almonds.

Legend has it that on December 13, 1764, a gentleman in Sweden was roused in the middle of the night by a beautiful voice. He saw a young woman in white moving through his room singing. She had wings and was carrying a candle. That was Lucia the Saint. She brought light, food, and wine as comfort on what was, in the Gregorian calendar, the longest night of the year. We celebrate Saint Lucia on December 13. Children will walk with lit candles singing the beautiful Lucia carol and bringing the Lucia bread.

Swedish Lucia breads *(Makes 22)*

1½ ounces yeast
2 cups lukewarm milk
⅛ ounce saffron
Scant 1 cup butter, melted
2 pounds all-purpose flour
1 teaspoon salt
½ cup superfine sugar
⅓ cup raisins

FOR FINISHING
44 raisins
1 egg, beaten

DISSOLVE THE YEAST IN THE WARM MILK in a mixing bowl, then add the saffron and keep stirring until the mixture turns yellow. Add the melted butter. In a separate mixing bowl, sift together the flour and salt, then stir in the sugar and raisins.

POUR THE YEAST MIXTURE INTO THE DRY INGREDIENTS AND STIR until the dough comes cleanly from the edge of the bowl. Knead the dough on a floured counter for 10 minutes, until it is shiny but not sticky. Put the dough back in the bowl and let rise for 1½ hours at room temperature.

LIGHTLY KNEAD THE DOUGH AGAIN ON A FLOURED COUNTER. Divide into 22 equal pieces. Roll them into sausages then curl the ends so that each piece is shaped like the number eight. Put one raisin in the middle of each circle. Place the breads on baking sheets lined with parchment paper, cover with dish towels, and let rise again for 30 minutes.

PREHEAT THE OVEN to 350°F. Brush the risen breads with beaten egg. Bake for 20 to 25 minutes, or until golden brown all over. Let cool on a wire rack. Eat them as they are, or spread with cold butter.

Pork foreloin or "pork roast" is one of the most popular cuts of meat in Scandinavia, though this traditional cut is not as well known in other countries as it once was. Serve it with the crisp pork rind on top. The Waldorf salad is sweet and crisp and goes well with pork.

Pork with rosemary, thyme, and garlic *(Serves 6)*

1 lemon
3 rosemary sprigs
5 thyme sprigs
5 cloves garlic, minced
Salt and pepper
5½ pounds pork roast

PREHEAT THE OVEN to 400°F. Grate the zest from the lemon, then cut the lemon in half and slice it finely. In a mixing bowl, combine the zest, lemon slices, rosemary, thyme, garlic, salt, and pepper.

REMOVE THE PORK RIND IN ONE PIECE from the top of the roast, making sure that the fat stays with the rind. Score a diamond pattern on the top surface of the pork, then rub in the herb-lemon mixture. Put the piece of rind and fat back on top. Tie all the way along the roast with a long piece of kitchen string, then place in a roasting pan. Roast for 1 hour 40 minutes, or until an instant-read thermometer registers 175°F.

REMOVE THE PORK FROM THE OVEN and let rest for about 15 minutes so that the juices can settle throughout the meat. Remove the string and carve the meat into slices, making sure there is a piece of the crisp pork rind with every portion. If it is Christmas Eve, serve with traditional Roast Duck and Gravy (page 212), and Caramel Potatoes and Red Cabbage (page 214).

Waldorf salad *(Serves 6)*

½ pound grapes, seeded
1 cup walnuts, broken into bits
2 apples, cored and cubed
⅓ cup heavy cream

PUT THE GRAPES, WALNUTS, AND APPLES in a mixing bowl and stir.

IN A SEPARATE BOWL, whip the cream until it forms soft peaks then fold it into the salad. Serve as soon as possible.

You could serve this ham on Christmas Eve, or for Christmas lunch when it would be part of a large buffet with herring, salad, and potatoes. The ham could also serve as a roast with different salads, bread, and cheese. It goes well with the fall salads on page 176.

Swedish Christmas ham *(Serves 15 as part of a buffet)*

6½ pounds ham, either on the bone or boned and rolled

4 quarts water

GLAZE

2 egg yolks

1 cup bread crumbs

½ cup whole grain mustard

½ cup packed dark brown sugar

Pepper

PLACE THE HAM IN LARGE BOWL, cover with cold water, and let soak in the refrigerator for 12 hours.

PREHEAT THE OVEN to 250°F. Put the ham in a large roasting pan and add the water. Slowly roast in the oven for 3 hours and 15 minutes, or until a meat thermometer inserted in the ham reads 167°F.

MAKE THE GLAZE. Mix together all the glaze ingredients in a bowl. Remove the ham from the oven and let cool slightly. Raise the oven temperature to 425°F.

REMOVE THE RIND FROM THE HAM and score a diamond pattern in the top layer of fat. Brush the glaze over the ham and return to the oven. Roast for 10 minutes, or until the ham is golden brown. Let cool before serving.

CHRISTMAS DINNER. This is a lovely meal that you could serve on other days of the year as well. For my family's Christmas dinner, I also cook the roast pork and Waldorf salad (page 208), and serve with red currant jelly. It is a real feast.

Roast duck *(Serves 4)*

1 free-range duck
Salt and pepper
1 crisp apple, cored and cubed
4 ounces prunes

PREHEAT THE OVEN to 400°F. Pour boiling water over the duck. Rub the inside of the duck with salt and pepper. Mix the apple and prunes together and put them in the cavity of the duck. Close the cavity with a trussing needle. Season the outside with salt and pepper.

PLACE THE DUCK ON A RACK and place the rack in a roasting pan. Roast for 2½ hours, or until the legs fall off easily. Let the duck rest for 10 minutes. Raise the oven temperature to 450°F.

CARVE THE DUCK INTO 10 PIECES, place in a baking dish, and return to the oven for 10 minutes. Serve the duck with the apple-prune mixture and the gravy (below).

Gravy *(Serves 4)*

DUCK STOCK
2 duck legs
3 cups red wine
4 cups water
1 carrot
1 onion, unpeeled
10 thyme sprigs
1 tablespoon peppercorns
1 tablespoon coarse salt

GRAVY
4 tablespoons butter
2 tablespoons all-purpose flour
1¼ cups heavy cream
2 teaspoons red currant jelly
Salt and pepper

MAKE THE STOCK. Pan-fry the duck legs in a large saucepan, turning occasionally, until they are golden brown. Add the red wine, water, carrot, onion, thyme, peppercorns, and salt. Bring to a boil, then reduce the heat and simmer for 2 hours, or up to 4 hours if you have time.

STRAIN THE STOCK USING A STRAINER and discard the duck and vegetables. Pour the broth into a container and let cool, then cover and store in the refrigerator overnight. Before use, scrape all the duck fat from the surface and save it for cooking Red Cabbage (page 214).

MAKE THE GRAVY. Melt the butter in a saucepan. Add the flour and stir until the paste comes away from the edge of the pan. Add 3 cups stock a little at a time, stirring after each addition until there are no lumps left. Bring slowly to a simmer, stirring constantly.

STIR IN THE CREAM and red currant jelly. Season with salt and pepper and keep warm until ready to serve.

This may seem an unusual way of cooking potatoes, but as far as my children and I are concerned, Christmas isn't Christmas without caramel potatoes. Another essential side dish is red cabbage. Its wonderful, sweet-sour-spicy flavor goes well with duck. I think the taste improves when it is prepared the day before serving.

Caramel potatoes *(Serves 4 to 6)*

2 pounds small new potatoes
¾ cup superfine sugar
3½ tablespoons butter

BOIL THE POTATOES IN A LARGE POT of salted water until tender, then drain. Once they are cool enough to handle, peel and let cool (this can be done the day before serving).

SHORTLY BEFORE SERVING CHRISTMAS DINNER, melt the sugar in a large sauté pan. When it is golden brown, add the butter and let the mixture simmer until it becomes a caramel, stirring as little as possible.

ADD THE POTATOES and gently turn them in the caramel until it starts to stick to them—this will take time, so be patient.

Red cabbage *(Serves 4 to 6)*

¼ cup duck fat
½ red cabbage, cored and thickly sliced
1 whole yellow onion
¾ cup red wine
½ cup superfine sugar
¼ cup red currant jelly
¼ cup vinegar or brine from pickled beets
1 cinnamon stick
10 whole cloves
Salt and pepper

MELT THE DUCK FAT IN A LARGE SAUCEPAN OR CASSEROLE, add the cabbage, and sauté over medium heat until shiny—don't let it brown.

ADD THE REMAINING INGREDIENTS and season with salt and pepper. Cover and simmer for 2 hours, or until dark purple and shiny. Remove the onion and season with additional sugar, salt, and pepper.

This is my favorite dessert for Christmas Eve. When serving it, you also play a little Christmas game. The rice pudding is served in a large bowl. Just before you take it to the table, add one whole almond and stir so nobody knows where it is. Everybody eats until someone finds the almond. You are allowed to cheat and hide the almond from the others if you find it, because the point of the game is to make the others keep eating while trying to find the almond. In the end, when the winner can no longer hide that he or she has the almond, he or she receives a present. Make the rice pudding and the cherry sauce the day before serving.

Rice pudding with warm cherry sauce *(Serves 6)*

RICE PUDDING
6 cups whole milk
2 vanilla beans
1¼ cups short grain rice
1 teaspoon salt
2 tablespoons superfine sugar
1 cup blanched almonds
¾ cup heavy cream

CHERRY SAUCE
1½ pounds pitted cherries, fresh, frozen, or in brine
1 cup superfine sugar
1 vanilla bean
2 cups water
3 tablespoons cornstarch

MAKE THE PUDDING. Gently heat 5½ cups of the milk in a large saucepan. Slit one of the vanilla beans lengthwise, without cutting it all the way through. Just before the milk starts to boil, add the rice and the slit vanilla bean. Cook gently for 30 minutes, stirring slowly and frequently so that it doesn't burn. Remove the pan from the heat and add the salt. Cover and let stand for 10 minutes. Remove the lid, stir in the sugar, and let cool (or until the next day).

REMOVE THE VANILLA BEAN and transfer the rice mixture to a large bowl. Chop the almonds coarsely except for one, which you save for the game. Whip the cream in a bowl until it forms soft peaks. Slit the second vanilla bean lengthwise and scrape out the seeds with the tip of a knife. Add them to the rice. Gently fold in the remaining ½ cup milk, then fold in one-third of the whipped cream. When the mixture is smooth, fold in the rest of the whipped cream and the chopped almonds. Taste the pudding: it should be sweet with a flavor of vanilla. Spoon the pudding into a serving bowl and hide the almond. Cover and place the bowl in the refrigerator.

MAKE THE CHERRY SAUCE. Put the cherries in a pan with the sugar, vanilla bean, and water. Bring to a boil, then reduce the heat and simmer for 15 minutes. Dissolve the cornstarch in enough water to make a thin paste and slowly add it to the cherry sauce, stirring constantly until it thickens and comes slowly to a boil. Taste and add more sugar if necessary but do not make it too sweet because the rice pudding is very sweet and the cherry sauce should add some acidity to it.

SHORTLY BEFORE you are going to serve the rice pudding, reheat the sauce and serve it on the side in a bowl.

SMÅKAGER: CHRISTMAS COOKIES. Vanilla butter cookies are the best in the world—crisp with the taste of real vanilla—and the swirl cookies have the added taste of chocolate. Be sure to make enough to last the entire Christmas vacation! The marzipan nougat delights are easy to make with children. Try cutting them into different shapes and covering them with chocolate.

Crisp vanilla Danish butter cookies *(Makes 80)*

Scant 1¾ cups butter
1¼ cups superfine sugar
1 egg
2 vanilla beans
3½ cups all-purpose flour

CREAM THE BUTTER AND SUGAR TOGETHER IN A BOWL until pale and fluffy. Add the egg and continue beating. Split the vanilla beans lengthwise and scrape out the seeds with the tip of a knife. Stir them into the flour, then fold all the dry ingredients into the butter mixture. Wrap the dough in plastic wrap and chill for 2 hours.

PREHEAT THE OVEN to 400°F. Roll the dough into very thin sausages about 2 or 2½ inches long. Curl each one into a ring and press the ends firmly together. Place on a baking sheet lined with parchment paper. Bake for about 8 minutes, or until lightly browned. Cool on a wire rack. Store the cookies in an airtight tin; do not mix them with other types of cookies or they will go soft.

Swirl butter cookies *(Makes 120)*

1¼ cups butter
1½ cups confectioners' sugar
1 egg
Scant 3 cups all-purpose flour
Scant 1 cup unsweetened cocoa powder
1 egg, beaten

CREAM THE BUTTER AND CONFECTIONERS' SUGAR TOGETHER with an electric mixer until pale and fluffy. Add the egg and beat well, then stir in the flour. Divide the dough in half and add the cocoa to one portion, working it until fully combined.

PREHEAT THE OVEN to 400°F. Roll both pieces of dough out into rectangles. Brush the pale dough with some of the beaten egg then cover it with the chocolate dough. Starting from a long side, roll up the dough to form a cylinder with a swirl pattern inside.

CUT THE CYLINDER INTO THIN SLICES and put them on a baking sheet lined with parchment paper. Glaze with the rest of the beaten egg. Bake for 8 minutes, or until golden brown. Remove from the oven and cool on a wire rack.

Chocolate marzipan delights *(Makes 45 to 50)*

14 ounces Homemade Marzipan (page 72)
Confectioners' sugar, for dusting
7 ounces milk chocolate, melted

CUT THE MARZIPAN IN THREE and roll out one piece on a counter dusted with confectioners' sugar until the marzipan is about ¼ inch thick. Place half of the melted chocolate on top of the rolled marzipan to cover it.

ROLL OUT THE SECOND PIECE OF MARZIPAN as before and lay it on top of the melted chocolate, followed by the remaining chocolate. Roll out the final piece of marzipan and lay it over the stack so that you end up with a total of five layers alternating marzipan and chocolate.

CUT INTO SMALL DIAMOND SHAPES and serve, or store in an airtight box and serve within 3 days.

Glossary

AQUAVIT. This traditional Scandinavian alcohol can be made from potatoes or grains, depending on which is most economical. The choice does not have any influence on the taste, which is the result of the herbs and berries that are added. Aquavit is served in specially designed glasses with lunch or dinner. The most famous brands are Linie Aquavit (Norway), Rød Aalborg and Jubiläums (Denmark), and OP Anderson (Sweden). In Denmark we also have a new high-end brand called Schumacher. Many Scandinavians still make their own aquavit with a variety of herbs and berries.

BEER. A wide range of beer is produced in Scandinavia. In the last ten years numerous microbreweries have opened. They bring new and exciting flavors to beer. Carlsberg has also developed a special range of beers named after JC Jacobsen, the founder of the company. They taste very nice and are perfect with marinated meat or poultry.

BEETS. This root vegetable can be round or cylindrical and is available in both summer and winter varieties. Beets have a sweet taste and are commonly preserved and served as a condiment with meat dishes. However, they are also good baked and eaten raw in salads.

BUTTERMILK. This is made by adding special bacteria to nonfat or low fat milk, giving it a slightly thickened texture and longer flavor. It is very useful for baking and makes a healthy drink that is delicious served cold.

CARAWAY SEEDS. These tiny dark-colored seeds look like cumin but have a very different taste. In Scandinavia caraway seeds are typically used in aquavit, bread, and cheese; I also use them in salads and stews.

CARDAMOM. The Swedes traditionally use this spice in cakes, buns, and bread, but also in ground meat mixtures. It is available ground, but I prefer to buy the green pods and grind them just before use.

COWBERRIES. Very small red berries, rather like small cranberries, cowberries are called lingonberries in the United States. They grow wild on bushes in the woods and are picked in late summer or early fall. They are quite sour and have a very high vitamin C content. Cowberries are traditionally made into cordial, or boiled with sugar to make lingonsylt—in Sweden it is a must to have lingonsylt with your meatballs. Cranberries can be substituted if you can't find any lingonberries.

CRÈME FRAÎCHE. Scandinavians learned to use this type of sour cream from the French. It is often served with cakes and tarts and used in dressings and cold sauces. In Scandinavia crème fraîche is available in various different fat levels from 9 to 38 percent fat. In the United States, reduced fat sour cream is used instead.

ELDERFLOWERS. These grow in woods, wasteland, or gardens, the seeds being widely spread by birds. They grow in most of Europe and the Middle East. In Scandinavia, they bloom in June and July. Pick the flowers early in the day, because once they open toward the sun they lose much of their pollen, plus there will be insects around them. Try to pick in the least polluted place possible, and never alongside roads with heavy traffic.

HAM. In Scandinavia cured ham is soaked in water then either baked or boiled. When served for dinner, it is often baked with a glaze of brown sugar and mustard. Different cuts of pork are used for ham in different parts of Scandinavia, some with the bone, others boneless.

HERRING. For thousands of years in Scandinavia, herring have been both basic food and served for more festive occasions. When caught they are salted and stored in large sealed buckets so that they last a long time. When you want to eat them, you soak them in water to remove the salt. You can also eat fresh herring fillets fried in butter, and buy them smoked, but the most common way to enjoy herring in Scandinavia is marinated. Shads are the largest member of the American herring family and live in the Atlantic Ocean. They are different to other herrings in that they travel from their saltwater homes to spawn in freshwater rivers. This fish is good boiled, broiled, and baked. If you are unable to buy shad, then you can use mackerel or freshwater bass instead.

HORSERADISH. Horseradish is a long root that grows underground. You can buy it fresh and grate it yourself, or buy it ready-grated. Preserved horseradish is fine for dressings and sauces. If you have a fresh root, store it in the refrigerator in plastic wrap; it is best grated just before cooking or eating.

JERUSALEM ARTICHOKES. A winter root vegetable, Jerusalem artichokes have a nutty taste and are very crunchy when eaten raw. They are suitable for salads, soups, and can be served baked or boiled.

LOVAGE. Lovage is a herb grown in Scandinavian backyards year-round. It has a very sharp taste and should be used judiciously. Salads, dressings, chicken stews, and garnishing are some of its best uses and, unlike some other herbs, lovage does not lose its flavor when cooked.

MARZIPAN. The quality of marzipan depends on the quantity of almonds it contains. Look for marzipan with an almond content of at least 60 percent; the color should be golden instead of white, and the texture should be soft and shiny. If you cannot get hold of good quality marzipan, you can always make it yourself (page 72).

MUSTARD. Many different kinds of mustard are enjoyed in Scandinavia. We have one for fish sauces that is grainy and has a sweet taste; another variety is more like Dijon mustard—very strong and a bit sour. Whole mustard seeds are also used for preserves and marinated herring.

OILS AND FATS. When cooking I mostly use olive oil and butter, for both taste and health reasons. When baking, it has to be butter to get the best result and flavor; for pan-frying I very rarely use butter and instead choose olive oil or some other kind of vegetable oil. I also favor olive oil for making salad dressings and marinades.

POTATOES. Potatoes are very important in the Scandinavian diet and can be eaten at almost every hot meal. Many different kinds are grown in different parts of the region. New potatoes are very popular and harvested around midsummer. They are best boiled within 24 hours of being harvested, and on those occasions should be eaten with cold butter and salt only.

POTATO FLOUR. Starch derived from potatoes and made into a flour is a very complicated chemical process. In Scandinavia it is widely used both for baking and thickening sauces. Often cornstarch can be used in its place.

RED CURRANTS. Small red berries that grow in small clusters on bushes both wild and in backyards. In season in Scandinavia in July and August, red currants have a fresh, sweet taste but can be a bit sour. They are eaten fresh on cakes and in fruit salads, or shaken with sugar to eat in the morning. Red currants are also made into jellies and lemonade right after picking.

RYE BREADS. The foundation of the famous open sandwich, these loaves have rye flour as their main ingredient. In Scandinavia they are often made with sourdough starter. Honey, malt flour, and different grains can be added to vary the flavor and texture.

RYE FLOUR. Flour made from rye grains. I prefer to buy rye flour from small organic producers. It should not be more than two months old, even if the package says the flour can last up to a year.

SALMON. Salmon lives in both salt and fresh water. It is a fatty fish yet very firm, easy to handle, and cook. It has become part of our everyday kitchen. You can eat it raw, marinated, fried, gravad ("buried"), or smoked. When you buy fresh salmon the color should be bright, the smell fresh, and the surface of the flesh clean and not slimy.

SOURDOUGH STARTER. Used for traditional rye breads in particular. In Scandinavia sourdough starter can be bought ready-made in specialty stores and health food stores, but you can also make it yourself from yeast.

SPELT. This ancient grain dates back to the Roman Empire and is related to wheat. The flour is popular in Scandinavia because it has a very nice taste, is easy to work with, and is perfect for bread and buns.

TROUT. If I want to steam fish, rainbow trout from Norway is my favorite, and I prefer it to salmon. The meat is firm and tender with a fresh sweet taste. I recommend buying and cooking it whole, rather than in fillets.

VINEGAR. We generally use a plain, clear distilled vinegar for brines and to enhance the flavor of dishes when cooking. It is also used for housekeeping tasks such as cleaning and stain removal.

YEAST. Fresh yeast is a staple in Scandinavian supermarkets. Baking is still part of daily life in many households, especially in the countryside. Even people who do not bake often will bake for birthdays and the Christmas festivities. Fresh yeast is favored for pastry and cakes as well as bread, but dried yeast can be substituted: for each ounce of fresh yeast, $2\frac{1}{4}$ teaspoons active dry yeast or $1\frac{1}{2}$ teaspoons instant yeast.

YOGURT. Scandinavia produces a wide range of different yogurt products with varying fat contents. They are used for breakfast, drinks, snacks, dressings and desserts.

WEBSITES WHERE YOU CAN FIND OUT MORE ABOUT SCANDINAVIA AND ITS FOOD PRODUCTS

TRAVEL
www.visitcopenhagen.com
www.visitnorway.com
www.visitdenmark.com
www.visitsweden.com

AQUAVIT
www.arcusbeverage.com

BEER
www.nogne-o.com

CHEESE
www.st-clemens.dk
www.jarlsberg.com

RETAILERS (U.S.)
www.scandiafood.com
www.scanspecialties.com
www.scandinavianfoods.net
www.williams-sonoma.com

MISCELLANEOUS
www.royalcopenhagen.com
www.TrinaHahnemann.com

Index

Acknowledgments

It has been a wonderful journey writing this book and I have a lot of people to thank for helping me make it happen. Firstly, an enormous thanks to Anne Furniss for taking on the project and for believing in me, and also to her and Helen Lewis for creative meetings and for being so responsive during 2007. Thanks also to all the other talented people at Quadrille. Thanks to Stig Jensen, the chef in Snapstinget, Copenhagen, and the staff there for wonderful and inspiring lunches served throughout the process.

Thanks to Lars Ranek for some wonderful trips around Scandinavia where we had a great time and where he took some beautiful pictures, and to Vibeke Kaupert for helping to put this book together.

I would also like to thank my mother for her support and a lot of hard work helping me in the kitchen with trying out recipes, and cleaning up after long days in the photographic studio! Also thanks to my friend Lisa Høgh Nielsen for helping me in the kitchen at all hours, to my soul mate in food Sonja Bock for going through my ideas, and my sister Silla Bjerrum for her encouragement and sharing her network.

Special thanks to the Dr. Holms Hotel in Norway for their hospitality. Finally, thanks to my husband Niels Peter for wonderful support and for never really tiring of all the cooking, litter, and cleaning up. Thanks for working with me into the long hours and for reading through drafts of the book again and again.